C000113546

YOU BRAND

A Manual for Confidence

YOU
BRAND

A Manual
for Confidence

Julia Goodman

Copyright © 2021 Julia Goodman
Line drawings by Mark Mason-Jones
Author photo by Susie Mackie
Book design by CHK Design

You brand and Performance Energy are registered trademarks.

The moral right of the author has been asserted.

Apart from any fair dealing for the purposes of research or private study,
or criticism or review, as permitted under the Copyright, Designs and
Patents Act 1988, this publication may only be reproduced, stored or
transmitted, in any form or by any means, with the prior permission in
writing of the publishers, or in the case of reprographic reproduction
in accordance with the terms of licences issued by the Copyright
Licensing Agency. Enquiries concerning reproduction outside those
terms should be sent to the publishers.

Matador
9 Priory Business Park,
Wistow Road, Kibworth Beauchamp,
Leicestershire LE8 ORX
Tel: 0116 279 2299
Email: books@troubador.co.uk
Web: www.troubador.co.uk/matador
Twitter: @matadorbooks

Paperback ISBN 978 1838593 568
Hardback ISBN 978 1838593 575

British Library Cataloguing in Publication Data.
A catalogue record for this book is available from the British Library.

Printed and bound by CPI Group (UK) Ltd, Croydon CRO 4YY

Matador is an imprint of Troubador Publishing Ltd

For my grandchildren
Jasmine, Lily and Ralph.
Be yourselves!

'Energy is Eternal Delight.'

William Blake

Testimonials

"Julia and the 'You brand' experience changed my life. Her programme and insight gave me the tools and confidence to 'perform' in front of large audiences that previously would have created anxiety. But it was way more than that – her warmth, insight and caring directness helped me to connect with who I am and to be proud of showing my own vulnerability and authenticity. You brand is a must for anyone who wants to communicate more of themselves, with passion. This book is a great place to start."
Kerry Dryburgh, Executive Vice President People & Culture and Chief People Officer, BP

"Have you ever felt intimidated by making a business pitch, going for an important interview or, in general, trying to make a good impression? If the answer is Yes then this book is a compelling and 'must read', as it explains the craft of communication and maps a very clear learning journey for all who aspire to grow, develop and create a long-lasting positive impression, wherever and whenever – whether in the traditional physical environment or indeed in the 'new normal' world of telepresence."
Mick Sweeney, CEO PineBridge Investments Ireland

"Julia Goodman is a true master of personal branding. Her approach helped me overcome my concerns that being dyslexic meant I could not speak in public, and she has coached staff at my private equity firm in presentation skills for many years. This is a must-read manual if you're seeking a confidence boost in your personal or professional life."
Guy Hands, Founder and Chairman of Terra Firma Capital Partners

"It's ironic that You brand is 'transformative', because it's our authentic self that we find, learn to express, to be, to speak, to breathe, to live. An investment that has no price."
Amy Burke, Director Group Human Resources, Vhi Healthcare

"The work of a lifetime encapsulated in a single volume. The author's unique insights, peppered with wit and wisdom, lead one on a remarkable journey of self-discovery and empowerment."
Simon David Eden MA Dist (RCA), playwright, screenwriter, novelist, member of the Writers Guild America West & The Society of Authors

"When I started at the Bristol Old Vic Theatre School in the seventies, it seemed to me to be a training for life, not just for acting. I remember thinking 'everyone should have this opportunity'. Some of us heeded the idea better than others, but hey, Daniel Day-Lewis didn't get the David Archer gig.

This book gives everyone that opportunity. 'Oh no, not another actor telling us how we can secure that contract by imagining we are a tree,' you might think. Well no, it's not. Julia Goodman goes out of her way, in a friendly, intelligent, extremely well written book, to emphasise that she's 'not trying to turn you all into luvvies'. If being a 'luvvie' means an over-the-top, narcissistic, false, fake show off, which I think it may do to some, then *You brand: A Manual for Confidence* is the very opposite. Everyone has a story to tell, everyone is unique, and what this book does is to bring out the truth of who you are and what your story is, because truth and honesty generate trust, and trust, let's face it, leads to sales. Unless of course you're Donald Trump, in which case absolutely none of this applies. The Donald's book, 'Twenty Thousand Lies, And Still The Suckers Vote For Me', will be on the shelves next to this one. I do urge you to make the right choice!"
Tim Bentinck, actor & author, David Archer in *The Archers* (BBC Radio 4)

"Julia Goodman's 'You brand' method surpasses all other forms of communication coaching. I have seen it transform the capability of accomplished presenters as well as people for whom presenting is terrifying. The method is hard but enormously impactful because it is authentic. While the best way to learn (and the most fun) is with Julia and her team, the book is a comprehensive substitute that walks through the steps and the method – or it can serve as a reference tool."
Alexandra Hess, Partner, Head of Investor Relations, Cinven

"This book is a masterclass in helping people to be themselves and in doing so communicate powerfully. It sets out a clear methodology to achieve your 'You brand'. I have seen from the beginning of Julia's business to today how her work builds personal leadership brands and compelling leadership performance.
This is why this is a book to read, re-read and then read again"
Neil Sherlock CBE, Non Executive Chair, Echo Research, former partner at KPMG and PwC

"I have worked with Personal Presentation over almost three decades across a variety of industries and roles. Their work does two things startlingly well: it gives the client the tools to liberate themselves from the often deadening constraints of modern business behaviour (such as PowerPoint) and at the same, enables them to tap into a deeply empowering energetic self - their 'You brand'. The results of this process are little short of transformative. One learns literally to perform oneself. One learns to connect with an audience in a profoundly human way. Business presentations cease to be a chore or a trauma and become instead a form of authentic self-expression. This stuff is dynamite!"
Stephen Jolly, Executive Director, M&C Saatchi

"It's more than a skill for life, this coaching has woken me up to the fact that in order to get anywhere and connect with anyone, in a truly meaningful way, I have to own what I'm doing and why I'm doing it. In short, I have to be me! It's safe to say You brand will not just help me with my future career, it has and will continue to help me be me."
Tom Gardner, Child Advocate and Education Researcher

"The improvement I have seen in my confidence and public speaking skills following my day with Julia is immeasurable. I always felt as if I had a lot to say but I struggled to convey it in an effective manner – which ultimately led to me struggling to land a graduate role. Julia helped me to combat this lifelong problem of mine and I have now managed to land my dream role with my dream company. I cannot thank her enough."
Amaan Abdulrahman, investment banker, economics graduate, Arsenal fan, World kickboxing champion. Featured in *How to Break into the Elite* (BBC Two, 2019)

"You 'remoulded' me to be me, and made a huge and positive difference in my life. You stand out in my career as the person who made the biggest lasting difference. Thank you with all my heart."
Des Crowley, speaking as CEO, Bank of Ireland UK

"You brand is a transformational, life changing, radical intervention on how you 'occur' to others and that has transformed the real me on the inside to being me on the outside."
Jon Harris, EVP Upstream, Sasol, and formerly EVP Technical, BG Group.

"The best advice is often the most simple and straightforward, you wonder why you didn't see it yourself. This book simply unlocks the potential already within you. For many years I presented as the professional I thought people wanted and expected to see. It was exhausting, often miscalculated and ultimately ineffective. Julia gets this and working through 'You brand' has helped me learn how to just be myself, which is especially critical in this new virtual world we are living in. It takes a lot of courage but the reward of being comfortable in your own skin and building deeper, stronger professional (and personal) relationships is well worth the journey."
Anthony D'Souza, Private Equity executive and fundraiser

"You helped me to reframe my internal monologue on my career motivations, which has given me the ability to speak passionately and authentically about who I am and what I add."
Elisabeth Sullivan, Group Legal Manager, INEOS

"It has never been more important for leaders to connect emotionally with others, by bringing our true selves to light. Practising with the tools Julia provided me has helped me move from anxiety to performance, and to start unlocking a more confident version of myself."
Tom Fuller, Vice President Wells, North Sea and Asia Pacific, BP

"This isn't coaching. It's liberating souls. For me what sets You brand apart from all the other approaches is that it is, by definition, different for everyone. In my personal experience when I first met Julia and her team I was struggling with a not unfamiliar dilemma around how much my relative success was down to the reputation of the company I worked for and how much was down to me. The transformation I experienced with Julia took me to a completely different place. I learnt that my dilemma was largely irrelevant.

Releasing my You brand and discovering how to present myself authentically enabled me to grow and develop and enjoy my professional and personal life fully.

I could now approach any prospect or situation with confidence. I also now derive more job satisfaction from my work than ever before, as well as believe that my advice and counsel become stronger every day. So much of that is thanks to Julia releasing my inner authenticity, for which I salute her and am eternally grateful."
David Telling, Founder & CEO, Telling Ltd

"As an award-winning presenter, I was comfortable with public speaking but knew something was missing and that I had reached a plateau without a way forward. Then, as part of a career transition, I decided to invest in my future and was fortunate to find Julia and the You brand course. The book echoes what you experience with Julia in person. It is not for those seeking a few quick tips to enhance existing skills but is perfect for those who are prepared to take a structured and proven route to discovering a more authentic version of themselves.

The steps are challenging and require honest reflection and feedback. However, the results are truly liberating, freeing you of inhibitions and enabling you to meaningfully engage with your audience, whoever or wherever they may be. In an age where technology dominates, the need to be authentically human and authentically You has never been greater. This book will guide you on the journey from knowing to doing and give you the ability to make a difference, however you choose to do so. I am really pleased that Julia has now made her wisdom and experience more widely available. The world desperately needs the communication skills that you will learn from this book."
David Wales MSc FRSA, Founder, SharedAim Ltd

Contents

Chapter Overview

Prologue

I've always considered myself extraordinarily lucky to have hit on the idea of You brand when I did. The corporate delayering during the recession of the early 1990s caused profound changes to many job descriptions. People in the worlds of finance, technology and engineering, whose focus for years had been on the detail, on getting the numbers right and the facts to stack up, suddenly found that they had to go out and win business, to present, pitch and negotiate, to sell their services and themselves. No longer could they just wait for the work to land in their laps. They needed new skills and the confidence to do a job that they had not signed up for.

The launch of my business in 1989 hit this wave perfectly. The skill of 'performing yourself', of selling yourself authentically and confidently, began to demand a high premium. Everyone I spoke to was eager to learn. The competition within the professional and financial services sector – the accountancy firms, banks, lawyers – was acute. And there was I, ready to jump with my big idea: simple, effective, releasing, enormously therapeutic, 'more of yourself – with skill'. The training could be applied to any situation and any arena, making introverted or shy people suddenly able to sell their enormous cognitive know-how to audiences large and small – something they would previously have shied away from – and giving extraverts the ability to 'have a chat' with a large audience, where they would normally have felt isolated and exposed. The confidence and joy they found in this achievement changed their lives and the fortunes of their businesses.

Over the last thirty years the **You brand** method has given people at all levels the confidence to realise their potential through self-awareness and self-belief, to bring the core of themselves to the fore and to find their true brand by expressing and communicating themselves, their unique selves.

When I started writing this book the world was a different place.

I am immensely proud of some of the things the work has achieved, more for what it represents for the individuals involved rather than any corporate advancement: increasing the pitch win rate of one of the Big Four advisory firms from 30% to 80% in one year; coaching prospective leaders to win promotion and inspire the loyalty and followship needed to do the job; giving thousands of individuals the confidence and the voice to be heard and seen for who they are and what they stand for; helping young people just starting out, unsure and uncertain that they count. All of this by learning to perform themselves, wherever they go.

When I started writing this book the world was a different place. Now a new normal of pandemic separates us from then. Thinking of how restricted our places of performance have become, I have wondered whether all the work I have been doing for years would still have immediate and simple relevance … small arenas, large arenas, conferences, presentations, meetings, interviews, anywhere and everywhere. Now that our homes and virtual communication platforms are the 'everywhere', would You brand coaching still be relevant? Rock up in front of your screen, sitting in your shorts on the end of the bed with a bowl of cereal in your hand …
The Millennials and Gen Z are doing this socially the whole time. Being interviewed on-line by a robot? Quite normal, happens a lot. So where does this 'performance' work come in now?

Human kind needs interaction and social stimulation. We need to connect. And that now needs a greater awareness and ability because of the technology that brings us together while standing between us. It's not good enough just to be technically savvy. We need to get ourselves across as the interesting, engaging, unique, authentic people that we truly are – all of us – using exactly the same methods that apply in the physical world, and that you will

learn in this book. Learning and practising the skill of performance – perhaps more than any other – will move you towards an infinite mind-set by developing in you attributes
of courage, optimism and resilience that will equip you to take on the unknown and the unforeseen.

> *'The most important factor is what performance
> does for people's confidence; it lifts people
> in ways that no other activity can.'*
> Gareth Malone, ground-breaking Choirmaster

Confidence is key, and it's fundamentally confidence that **You brand** is all about. Speaking truth to power, #metoo, Black Lives Matter, the growing awareness that we have the personal power to influence things ... all of this is overhauling the world we now live in, and when we have the confidence to be ourselves and express ourselves we can actually help make change happen.

Julia Goodman
October 2020

www.youbrand.com

The Driving Premise Of This Book

When we communicate, there's a gap between how we think we come over and how other people actually experience us.

We may be unaware of it because no-one tells us. And if they do, we don't know what to do about it. Or we feel they've got an agenda, or a personal perspective we don't agree with.

This 'perception gap' can have a negative impact on our presence, relationships, achievements, self-esteem and confidence.

It's unrealistic to try to eradicate this gap entirely, because everyone we meet will have an individual perspective on us. But **You brand** coaching will help you to reduce it and have greater self-awareness and control over the impact you make. Self-awareness brings choice; and choice, if we know how to exercise it, brings confidence.

You brand has two components: character, what makes you who you are – that's 'You' – and the ability to project and communicate that You consistently, wherever you go, whatever situation you're in – that's 'brand'.

No matter how exposed, judged and vulnerable you feel, You brand wraps you in a protective cloak that stops these feelings from distorting the way you come across and uses them as positive fuel.

This is a pioneering coaching methodology rooted in the psychology, discipline and techniques of the professional theatre. It's not about faking it or pretending to be something you're not. A true actor uses themselves to inform 95% of the character they are playing. The key to great communication is to use more of yourself, with skill. This is what a good actor does.

And that's why the skills and techniques of the theatre that run through this book will release that ability in you like nothing else.

You brand will give you an understanding and a practical toolkit to enable you to 'perform yourself' authentically, in all your uniqueness..

Succeeding in this performance challenge is one of the most satisfying achievements there is, and the confidence it brings you will permeate every aspect of your life.

I hope that this book will help you to accept and celebrate your individuality, and use it positively, everywhere.

Enjoy your adventure!

Introduction

In 1989, when I was forty-two, my life was pretty chaotic. I'd just finished a European tour playing Lady Macbeth. I was divorced, living alone with my two adolescent children, and when not working I was living on £90 a week social security.

Three years later my company, Personal Presentation Ltd, turned over its first million, and has since gone on to become an established leader in the field of communication coaching, transforming the careers and lives of thousands of people in the worlds of business, politics, academia and everyday life. So how did I get there?

When I was fourteen, the theatre came to town. My sleepy home town of Chichester in West Sussex, a beautiful cathedral city nestling between the Downs and the sea in the south of England. The pioneering and famous Chichester Festival Theatre, forerunner of the National Theatre, set me on my path for life. The theatre became a central focus for my family, which already had in its DNA creativity in many forms: my father was from a long line of painters and eccentric and creative entrepreneurs, with a strong dash of the Jewish outsider; in 1945 my working-class mother, straight out of the Land Army aged twenty-one, was recruited by Joan Littlewood as a founding member of Theatre Workshop (Joan later became my mentor and role model, and was a strong influence on me from a young age). Mum's stories of Rudolf Laban (the movement guru) and Ewan MacColl (with whom she sang) are some of my earliest formative memories.

The theatre was a gift to us and the community, bringing together a disparate group of people who dedicated themselves to raising the money and getting it built. There's an old saying that 'It takes a village to bring up a child'; in this instance, it took a small city to give birth to a major theatre. It brought together individual talents, abilities, dreams and aspirations into a shared passion that united the town and had a huge influence on our family. All I could think of was 'How can I be part of this?' My father sat on the development board of the theatre and became its chief design adviser (he designed the famous symbol of Minerva's head which adorns the façade of the studio theatre). This enabled him, with much pleading and begging from me, to get me (underage at fourteen) a summer holiday job as usherette, ice cream seller and, later, box office assistant.

The theatre had a big impact on many of my friends too. It gave them jobs as scene shifters, extras, dressers, dishwashers and waiters or waitresses in the restaurant. Many of them went on to have fine careers as actors, writers and directors: Mike Elphick (*Boon*), David Wood OBE (perhaps best known for his theatre shows and adaptations for children), Howard Brenton (playwright), Adrian Noble (director of the Royal Shakespeare Company), Anthony Andrews (*Brideshead Revisited*), Malcolm Stoddard (later to be my husband in *The Brothers*) and many more… including me!

What I saw on a nightly basis in those early days in the theatre at Chichester were extraordinary performances by wonderful actors in great plays, new and old, led and inspired by the charismatic Laurence Olivier. Joan Plowright, Michael Redgrave, Sybil Thorndike, Lewis Casson, Albert Finney, Tom Courtenay, Michael Gambon, Derek Jacobi, Maggie Smith, Robert Stephens, Jeremy Brett and many more, night after night, left me with a lasting impression of what quality and professional standards of performance really mean: that less is more, that emotional meaning is in the pause, that when truth comes from within it reaches and moves us, that clarity of meaning and purpose are not in the words but in how much you believe in and are moved by the character. I experienced close up just how brave and courageous the performer needs to be. And I knew that this was all I wanted to do – there was nothing else (I've often said to parents of aspiring actors who want their child to get some qualifications as a fallback that if you have a Plan B you don't have a Plan A – and I see that single-minded determination as a requirement for pursuing any dream, not just acting).

But the 'Aha!' moment for me – and my embryonic realisation of the relevance of the theatre to everyday life – came from something that happened to me at school. I went to a convent school – a small, not terribly exclusive or academic one in Bognor Regis. I failed the dreaded eleven-plus exam, so Villa Maria was the only alternative to the then untried, sprawling secondary moderns, as they were called then (the word 'secondary' never sat well with me!).

Villa Maria didn't have a drama department and never put on a school play. I was considered rather naughty, although I don't think it was naughtiness so much as a natural sense of fun, curiosity and hunger for life that would often get me into trouble. For example, during our lunch break my friends and I would go to the town's new Wimpy Bar to flirt with the talent from the local boys' school. I used to roll up my knee-length skirt to just below my (rather large) school knickers to follow the 60s miniskirt fashion, and stretch my hat out of shape to make it less convent and more St Trinian's, with my tie askew and my shirt half untucked with top buttons undone. Sophisticated and individual – or so I thought. God knows what I really looked like! All totally innocent, but my propensity to live in the moment and not give things a second thought meant that I frequently got caught while everyone else had covered their tracks. Because of antics such as this I spent a lot of time outside the study of the headmistress, Sister Laurence – a terrifying woman! She once asked the class who of us had kissed a boy. Sitting on the front row (so I could see the blackboard; I was very short-sighted), I shot my hand up – being the truthful girl I was – only to find as I looked round the class that I was the only one. I knew for certain that many of my classmates had gone a lot further than simply kissing, but I took the rap for everyone! This was an eye-opener for me, though it never stopped me speaking up. But it did get me into a lot of trouble, to the extent that Sister Laurence told my parents that I was the only pupil she'd ever wanted to strike! So as I approached fifth form I was rather surprised and thrilled to be made a senior prefect. This, I later realised, was a very canny move on Sister Laurence's part to 'rein me in' and redirect my energy by giving me responsibility.

Smoking had begun to creep into the school and was becoming a problem among the younger girls. I had previously regularly smoked on the journey between home and school, but when I became a responsible and concerned prefect (Sister Laurence's wheeze had worked!), I resolved to use my position of authority to do something about the smoking epidemic (and create a bit of drama into the bargain...). In order to make the most impact I gathered all the school into the assembly hall, stood up on the stage and lectured them on smoking and its dangers. As I stood there looking out at the sea of upturned faces I felt an extraordinary energy surge through me; I had the authority and the ability to command attention and communicate a strong message. This was not me as an actor (although I did later become one) but me as myself. I never forgot that feeling of sheer freedom of expression, the feeling of power and the electric charge between me and my audience. And I still feel this whenever I have

If you have a
Plan B you don't
have a Plan A
– I see that
single-minded
determination as
a requirement
for pursuing
any dream.

the occasion or need to address people. It resonated hugely with me and was what inspired me later, in part at least, to find a way to enable other people to feel that same thing and to command an audience.

From Chichester I went to drama school in London, learning from the best how to be. I was taught by Cicely Berry (one of the world's leading voice coaches), Litz Pisk (Head of Movement at the Royal Central School of Speech and Drama) and George Hall, pioneering head of Central and founder of the Poor School. I then became a professional actor and producer and spent twenty-seven years working in film, TV and on the stage, finding early fame in *The Brothers* and *The Lotus Eaters*. I learned comedy timing (and how to survive!) working with comics such as Ronnie Corbett, Frankie Howerd, Dick Emery, Alastair Sim and Leslie Phillips. I worked alongside Charles Dance, Trevor Howard, Claire Bloom, Simon Callow and many less well-known but wonderful actors and directors. I discovered I had directing and producing talent through my time running the British Actors Theatre Company with Kate O'Mara and Peter Woodward, and had the privilege of playing leading roles such as Rosalind in *As You Like It* and Mrs Sullen in the *Beaux' Stratagem*, and Lady Macbeth. So I had a wonderfully varied career: rep, fringe theatre, West End, television series, film, Shakespeare... a fabulous cradle of learning and experience.

Then when I was in my forties it all came to a grinding halt – a common experience for women actors. As Juliet Stevenson once said, 'Just as you're getting really good, nobody wants you!' The good, stretching parts began to dry up. I was divorced, bringing up two adolescent children on my own, which meant I could no longer go on tour or be away for any length of time. I wasn't getting any parts that really stimulated me. I was getting bored with being just a jobbing actor.

I wanted something more. And I desperately needed money. Something had to change. Me! Lying in the bath – and there must be a reason that Archimedes shouted 'Eureka!' in the bath, not the laboratory* – I had the idea of taking my lifelong skills, learned and innate, in communicating and performing into the world of business,

---

* There is! A warm bath releases dopamine in our brains, relaxes us and turns our attention inwards so we're more likely to make insightful connections; and it puts our conscious brain 'on hold' so our subconscious is free to work on finding a creative solution to a problem.

helping non-actors to draw on the psychology and discipline of the theatre and its 2,000 years of precise techniques and dynamics.

Things have changed a bit in more recent years, partly because of easier access to the technology that allows anyone to create images and films, from the spontaneous 'selfie' to a full-blown production on YouTube. People are less self-conscious – although the good old British reserve can still be a real challenge! But one of the more infuriating aspects of the arts at the time when I had my Eureka moment was the pervasive myth that they are the exclusive domain of professionals, and a closed shop to any outsider having the temerity to enter this special territory as anything other than an audience or admirer. Now I don't mean that an 'amateur' approach to a professional activity is acceptable; it isn't, because amateur and professional are very different in their expectations, aspirations and processes. But I did believe that it was entirely possible to coach 'outsiders' in what can feel like an abnormal process, and enable them to embrace a professional approach to the art of personal communication and performance – particularly in the business world, where the need and anxiety are generally greatest.

So that became my passion: to create a methodology to enable people to perform their true selves. This took me four years of intense thought drawing on all my experience as an actor, and a lot of sometimes hair-raising trial and error. In those early days I used unsuspecting clients as guinea-pigs and, quite frankly, winged it much of the time. I worked tirelessly until I'd got all the basic ingredients, processes and exercises worked out in a way that was clear and worked for non-actors, and was engaging and experiential, and they could see the results. And that was just Day 1 of the programme!

Working with my team to develop the **You brand** programme into what it is today was to be the focus of my professional life for the next twenty-five years.

This book is a result of that focus.

The structure of the book and how to use it

The book is based on my one-to-one **You brand** coaching programme, which I run over four or five days with a week or more between each session – for recovery and 'soak' time. It's impossible of course to replicate the full face-to-face experience through the written word, but you will get a good understanding of some of the key elements. So that you can follow a similar process, I recommend you work through the book in small chunks and at your own pace, allowing yourself time to digest intellectually, emotionally and physically – and to practise!

Throughout the book I include exercises that you can do in your kitchen or sitting room. Most of these you can do on your own using a camcorder or the camera in your mobile phone. For the more interactive exercises, it'd be ideal if you could enlist a trusted friend.

I've included a few icons to help with navigation:

 This denotes an exercise for you to do.

 I use a diary icon wherever I've included a personal anecdote.

 This 'head' icon marks a piece of relevant psychology or neuroscience.

Where I've included passages that are relevant but adjacent to the narrative, or are of particular significance, I've highlighted these with a colour wash so as not to disrupt the flow.

You may like to read through the whole book first to get an overview of it, and then go back and do the exercises once you've got it mapped out; or else use this same approach, but a chapter at a time.

I'd also urge you to start keeping a **You brand** diary. Use it to record your observations and experiences, and people's responses to you and yours to them, as you work through the book and try things out. You can do this as notes in your phone, or else buy yourself a pocket-sized notebook that you can keep with you. Keep it simple and quick, making a mental note of things in the moment; then write them down at the end of the day in a more reflective, relaxed place – sitting in bed or in the bath, for example. It will help keep you focused, raise your awareness and make your whole experience more proactive.

If you possibly can, please **do the exercises**! I know that with self-help books it's all too easy to skip over these, promising you'll come back to them later, but then don't. And even though you'll mainly be doing them on your own, you may feel self-conscious, at least to start with. But persevere and it'll become easier. If you actively engage in this way you'll get full value from the book and see real change in yourself. For some lucky people though, just having a different intellectual way of looking at things is all they need to make a change in how they behave or perform. If that works for you, then great! But I'm a firm believer that **there is a chasm that separates knowing from doing**. My objective for you with this book is to get you to *do*, so that you'll experience a real change in how you communicate and interact with people – rather than just knowing a load of theory!

The journey you'll be going on looks like this:

You
The journey starts with 'You' – how you are perceived by the outside world, and how the way you look and sound influences the way people feel about you. We'll look at whether the verbal and non-verbal messages you put across align with what you intend and how you feel about yourself – or not! After this initial assessment we'll start to work with a performance toolkit that will help you to bridge the gap between how people see you and how you see yourself, and to help you look and sound real, natural and engaging.

THE
JOURNEY
MAP °

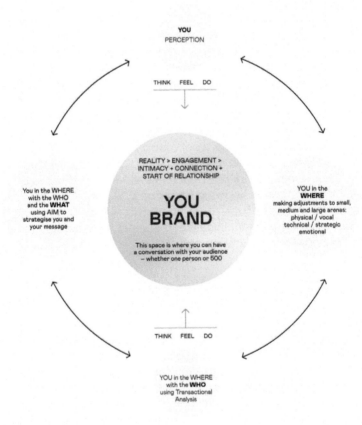

YOU
PERCEPTION

THINK   FEEL   DO

REALITY > ENGAGEMENT >
INTIMACY + CONNECTION +
START OF RELATIONSHIP

YOU
BRAND

This space is where you can have
a conversation with your audience
– whether one person or 500

You in the WHERE
with the WHO
and the **WHAT**
using AIM to
strategise you and
your message

YOU in the
WHERE
making adjustments to small,
medium and large arenas:
physical / vocal
technical / strategic
emotional

THINK   FEEL   DO

YOU in the WHERE
with the **WHO**
using Transactional
Analysis

Where

We'll take the reality and naturalness that you've begun to discover in the new, performing You, and look at how you can switch these on wherever you are, even in those places – or 'arenas', as I term them – where you may feel awkward (or you are unaware of what is happening to you and you are taken by surprise). For some people that may be in the large arena (making a speech at a conference, speaking at a dinner or standing up in front of a lecture hall), for others in the medium (presenting to the board or talking with a medium-sized group) or the small (a one-on-one chat over a coffee, a conversation or interview). And of course many of these have their parallel in the virtual world as well, which we'll be looking at in Chapter 11. We'll use the large arena (I take my clients onto a West End theatre stage for this. Don't worry; we won't be going) to explore the fuel of emotional connection, to push your performance 'envelope' and to give you some new techniques to work with: among them are 'kinaesthetics', a way of choreographing you and your message across the public, social and intimate spaces in order to make it as clear, engaging and powerful as possible. In the process we'll discover the laws of performance that all arenas have in common. This is great because it means you don't have to learn a load of different skills for different situations!

Who

Then we bring all this learning into play in conversation, and work with Transactional Analysis (TA), using a model that will help you understand and navigate the psychology of interactions so that you can get the best out of any situation. If you practise it and use it actively, the 'TA House' will have a big impact on your relationships with other people – and with yourself. It's a great model, one I think you'll get really hooked on. You'll read more about it in Chapter 12.

What

We'll work with 'Aimapping' (Audience/Arena Impact Mapping), which is a tool to help you 'strategise' your message and make sure that you're pressing the right buttons in the person/people you're speaking with, and pulling together all the lateral, emotional and physical information around the people and situation as well as the linear and intellectual aspects, so that you and your messages 'land'.

Towards the end of the book we'll focus on listening: how you listen now, and how to train yourself in and practise *active* listening, which will strengthen your influence in relationships by creating a feeling of shared understanding. Neuroscience is now telling us that we're not naturally programmed to listen, but only to 'take turns' in speaking – so that our instinctive focus is not on what the other person is saying, but on what we are going to say next (this may come as no surprise!). Listening is something we really do have to learn how to do. There will be some key learning here for you to process and use; and – as with everything you take from this book – you will need to practise actively in your day-to-day interactions in order to make the learning come to life and really stick. The two complementary processes of performing yourself and using TA and listening together will transform your everyday communication and relationships.

Please remember that this book is not a collection of random hints and tips but a *methodology*. All the ingredients are interrelated and support and develop each other (that's why the Journey Map is circular and all the parts link to each other backwards as well as forwards). They also build in a structured way; if you really want to work towards a fully rounded You brand, then I'd urge you to start at the beginning and work right through to the end.

But if you take nothing else from this book, there is one 'magic' ingredient I'll introduce you to that will transform the way you communicate. Practising and applying this one thing will bring about great change for you, because it's the foundation on which everything else is built. It will help enable you to master all situations and, like learning to ride a bike, it will eventually set you free.

CHAPTER 1

The Hero's Journey, Theatre and The Cliff

'That's not flying; that's just falling with style.'
Woody, *Toy Story*

The exploration you're about to embark on contains elements of the classic quest or hero's journey – which, as defined by American mythologist Joseph Campbell, is the story of the man or woman who, through undergoing great danger or suffering, experiences the true essence that lies beneath our physical world and returns from this eternal source with gifts powerful enough to set their society free.

Now it's not my intention to inflict great suffering on you, or to turn you into a heroic social reformer! But I do invite you to be the hero of this book, and to embark on a quest that will take you from your normal, familiar world into one that will probably often feel strange and abnormal. The object of this quest lies in the realm of perception and personal communication. The normal world is the everyday world familiar to us all: the world where personal communication – the way we speak and respond – is taken largely for granted, where the accepted wisdom is that good or charismatic communicators are born and not made, and where we generally have a low expectation of the power of the spoken word to move or inspire us in real life. That power we tend to think of as confined to films, plays and the occasional gifted communicator.

Our adventure will be into the world of the theatre, the world of professional performance, projection and communication. Theatre is the quintessential hero's journey. It shows us the essence of who we are in a cathartic way that allows us to grow. But the specific aspect of this hero's journey I want us to explore together – and which I lived for many years as an actor – is that made by the players on the stage: into the awareness, science, psychology, techniques and discipline that they have to adopt in order to inhabit the abnormal world of performance and make us, the audience, believe in this world and identify ourselves in it, so that we are lifted up and dropped back into our normality with a greater clarity and a heightened sense of purpose, being, skill and ability. On this journey you'll likely encounter different ways of seeing and thinking about things – and I'll encourage you to *do* them differently as well. You'll return to the 'normal' world equipped with a way of working and a set of powerful tools that can transform your everyday communication. This higher awareness and enhanced ability may change how you see the people around you, how they see you and how you see yourself, all of which will probably impact your life in all sorts of surprising, revelatory, challenging but ultimately positive ways.

All of this won't be without risk. It is exactly the same risk that actors face. Michael Powell, in his brilliant book *Acting Techniques*, puts it beautifully:

> *'The most technically accomplished and fearless performance won't truly connect unless it allows glimpses of the vulnerability that makes us all human, and this is arguably the greatest risk you can make as an actor... If you can find the courage to share these secrets with the world, you will be a compelling actor, because you will be truthfully human, with all the beauty and ugliness, contradictions and complexity, that this entails. This is a rare commodity indeed.'*

... a rare commodity that can be yours! I hope that this book will give you the self-awareness and techniques to allow you to be honest and courageous enough in your communication that you too can – when you wish to – reveal yourself confidently in all your humanity, and in so doing invite other people to explore theirs. This is the litmus test of great communication, and the beating heart of this book.

At the end of this adventure there's a great prize to be won, a pot of gold: your **You brand**, and all that goes with it, whether it's the slow realisation that you've changed and are stronger, or a more immediate transformation that enables you to manage your world better, with more confidence. Some of the normal adventures you've already been on might include getting your first job, leaving home, going on your first date, moving from being team member to team leader, changing career and following another path... These are all adventures in which you are the hero or heroine and must hack through the jungle of a new experience to get back to the normal world changed, enlightened, released and better able to deal with it.

Don't worry! Just because we're hitching a ride through the world of theatre doesn't mean I'm expecting you to put on a big performance somewhere or come out with something exceptional that has little connection with your everyday life. Sure, that particular experience will be invaluable to you if you have to make formal presentations or speak at the annual conference in front of hundreds of people. But you will see that the techniques, awareness and understanding you need for those 'big' places are *exactly the same* as in 'small' places too: conversations, close-up meetings, day-to-day interactions with people, whether in person or virtually.

And I certainly don't want to turn you into a 'luvvie', or into something you're not. Referencing the theatre and acting is about taking the skills and awareness of the professional performer and showing you how you can apply them to yourself, so that the way you communicate is more self-aware and has more colour, variety and impact.

While a bad actor hides behind the character they're playing, a good actor uses themselves to inform 95% of the role. Michael Sheen (*Frost/Nixon*, *The Damned United*, countless theatre roles) puts it succinctly: 'Ultimately I am just playing myself in different circumstances. So I look for what I might have in common with the character and then take that part of myself and just make it bigger.'

If you don't know it already, I hope you'll soon see that jt's not just OK to be you – it's one of the greatest gifts you can give to yourself and others, and is integral to any powerful communication.

The cliff
One of the analogies I like to share with clients is that of a first night in the theatre. I tell them that their presentations, pitches, meetings and so on are like a first night because more often than not they're one-offs, not to be repeated. In the case of a professional actor, by the time we get to first night, everything has been rehearsed and aligned to the event – script, direction, players, backstage support, lighting – we've worked on the delivery and execution to a high degree. Why? Because anything else means certain death! When we step on stage and look down, there, dizzyingly far below us, is the bottom of the cliff. We have to acknowledge the risk and

It's not
just OK to be you
– it's one of the
greatest gifts you
can give to
yourself and others,
and is integral
to any powerful
communication.

build in that fear and work with it. Think of a base jumper preparing to jump – you wouldn't do it unless you were trained and properly prepared, would you? For some reason though, when it comes to our personal communication, all of this common sense so often flies out of the window.

Some of us can't see the cliff and are in denial; or others just get to an OK place but never feel safe or able to really fly. Very few take it seriously and get the right training and support, so that they can start to feel the buzz of jumping and the confidence of knowing that they will land safely, and will want to do it again (while remaining mindful that the cliff is always there and always dangerous!).

Let's look at these responses in more detail. Think about which one resonates most with you.

Denial
You've jumped off the cliff before and it went horribly wrong – you had a crash landing – so now you avoid going to the top of the cliff at all. You look for somewhere to hide until the moment's passed. You become invisible in your organisation, or keep in the background, no matter how senior you are; you don't go to the party; or if you do you find making 'small-talk' awkward and uncomfortable, or you stand in a corner torn between wanting no one to notice you and hoping someone will. All of this can be very limiting in your career or social life.

Coping
You accept jumping off the cliff as an inevitable fact of life, something you have to do. You're not good at it but you find ways of coping, of getting through it. You're obviously uncomfortable making a speech, clinging to the podium and your script. You dread being asked to 'say a few words', or being the focus of a meeting. You stumble over your words, easily get thrown and lose your way – and your audience! Or at a party you force yourself to meet people, but you get tongue-tied, go red in the face and wish the ground would swallow you up – or you overcompensate and become a bore and scare people off! This is also all too common with virtual communication platforms (Zoom, MS Teams, Webex etc), where many people seem ready to settle for inadequate communication and impact – sometimes even resorting to turning their camera off.

Ability/managing
You jump off the cliff and you fly! You know what to expect and how to deal with it, and how to use your nerves to best effect. The whole

ABILITY: THE BUZZ!
You – free and able!
You can manage situations
and be proactive.

**COPING: BORING /
UNCOMFORTABLE**
Not You at your best:
no presence, no charisma.
Reactive.

OUCH!

DENIAL (AFTER THE CRASH LANDING!):
You in a dark place – playing an
avoidance game? Career and life limiting.

thing is such a satisfying and exhilarating experience that you actively seek out opportunities to jump again. People feed back to you how much they enjoyed that Zoom meeting with you, and how they left feeling energised and inspired. You become the company's spokesperson of choice, an able after-dinner speaker or top of the party invitation list. Or just more confident in every situation.

Past experience quickly shapes our attitude to things and plays a large part in determining our response to situations. I had a good experience, in my fifth-form days, when I addressed the school assembly on the dangers of smoking – a highly charged and untried scenario, but because it went well and I enjoyed it, I have felt positively attracted to that sort of experience ever since; by contrast, shortly after that I froze in a piano exam and sadly never took another one (more on this later). And that's what I want for you in your personal communication: to give you the tools so that you have a good experience, so that you are lifted up in a positive spiral that takes you higher and higher in terms of understanding, ability, effectiveness, confidence, self-belief.

Ultimately, mastering the art of personal communication can open the door to untold riches. I've always felt that much of what has been written on the subject is limited, in two ways. First, it confines the techniques of good communication to 'special' occasions: making a presentation or a speech, giving a TED talk, that sort of thing – and of course, these sorts of events are critical anxiety triggers. But in my experience, people don't easily make the link from there to other areas and miss the fact that the same skills can apply to everyday situations and interactions, where we're not just talking *at* people but *with* them: engaging them in conversation, interacting in meetings and social events, talking 'off the cuff' in our normal day-to-day lives – which is where most of us spend most of our time! And second, a lot has been written about the **what** rather than the **how** of communication: it describes what great communicators do and what it looks like on the outside, rather than letting you in on the secret of how they're doing it, of what's going on beneath the surface.

This book is about how you communicate in the real, everyday world. It includes models, exercises and hopefully some 'Aha!' moments that will help you in a very practical way to develop your impact and genuine presence, to be more visible, and to take on new challenges and higher-profile roles with more confidence (if that's what you want). I hope that by the end of it you'll feel free from the distortion that can come from the fear of not being liked, from the need to 'fit in', and that you'll feel happy to be recognised, accepted and respected for who you are. Being liked is a meagre ambition when you are free to be yourself and able to speak your truth to power.

If all of this sounds rather highfalutin and pretentious... well, time and again I've seen this coaching process gradually change how people feel about themselves and then how they see and relate to others. This comes from a growth in awareness, self-acceptance and confidence that 'it's OK to be you' and to celebrate that uniqueness. Doing this takes courage and skill, but it's a craft that you can learn. With practice it can change your life, and the lives of those around you.

SUMMARY CHAPTER 1

• The psychology, techniques and discipline of the professional theatre are very relevant to effective communication in everyday life.

• Showing vulnerability is essential to great acting – and to great communication.

• This book isn't about turning you into something you're not.

• Developing your personal communication is likely to change how you see people, how they see you and how you see yourself.

• There are three approaches to 'the cliff': denial, coping and managing.

• This book is about how you communicate in the everyday world, not just special occasions.

• Being a good communicator is a craft you can learn, but it takes courage and skill.

• It's not about being liked, but having the confidence to be accepted as who you are. This is the foundation for personal development and growth.

Things to work on
Reflect. Then read on!

CHAPTER 2

Perception
is Reality

*'O wad some Power the giftie gie
us, to see oursels as ithers see us!'*

Or, in modern English:
*'Oh would some Power the gift give us,
to see ourselves as others see us.'*
Robert Burns

In just about every situation – some of them hugely important to our success and happiness – we are judged by how we come across to people. The way people see us is what, for them, defines who we are: rightly or wrongly, **perception *is* reality**. But the scary fact is that the way we see ourselves and the way others perceive us can be hugely different. We may have great qualities, noble intentions, be thoroughly decent people, have done some splendid things; but unless these qualities are visible, unless we can communicate them through the impression that we convey of ourselves, they can easily go unnoticed or be open to interpretation.

Being 'open to interpretation' means that, if we don't express and project ourselves congruently and convincingly, people may get a distorted or wrong sense of who we are. They are unlikely to get the impression of us that we want, and will be left to make up their own minds about who we are and how they feel about us. This is particularly the case when meeting people for the first time, in that all-important moment of making a first impression; but even when we know someone well, the way we come over continues to have a strong influence on their perception and their emotional reaction to us. And we can have much more control over this than we may think!

The consequence of how we are experienced can be huge, for one very simple reason: the way people feel about us impacts on how they feel about themselves in our presence. If we look bored or sound depressed, for instance, people can easily infer that it is they who are boring or depressing. So they're unlikely to want to spend a lot of time hanging out with us, are they? The reverse is also true of course!

Before a client comes to me for the first time, I ask them to fill out a 'Personal Profile' form that gives them a chance to put into simple words the situations and challenges, both positive and not so positive, that they regularly come up against. Please spend a few minutes thinking about and answering these questions, and write your answers down on the form below or in your **You brand** diary:

Personal Profile

1. YOUR NAME

2. COMPANY / ORGANISATION / SITUATION

3. JOB TITLE / RESPONSIBILITIES

4. AGE (OPTIONAL!)

5. HOW DO YOU SEE YOURSELF?

6. HOW DO YOU THINK OTHER PEOPLE SEE YOU?

7. DOES THIS CHANGE DEPENDING ON THE SITUATION YOU'RE IN? HOW?

8. WHAT TYPES OF INTERACTION DO YOU FIND MOST CHALLENGING?
(e.g. work: with colleagues; with 'senior' people; delivering and receiving open
and honest performance feedback; interactions/negotiations with clients,
suppliers, advisers... Social/home/personal life: 'difficult' conversations
with friends, spouse, partner, children; social situations; making speeches...)

9. WHAT HAPPENS TO YOU IN THESE SITUATIONS?
(e.g. how do you feel, how do you think you behave?)

10. WHAT WOULD YOU MOST LIKE TO GET OUT OF THIS PROGRAMME/BOOK?

 You may like to show the form and your answers to someone else to get their view; they may see you differently from how you imagine they do, and probably quite differently from how you see yourself! It's an invaluable perspective to have.

Over the years I've had some interesting responses, ranging from 'Nobody sees me the way I really am' right through the spectrum to 'Everyone sees me in exactly the same way I see myself!' In my experience, neither extreme is accurate; but this 'perception gap' is something we are all vulnerable to.

This questionnaire is significant because it is the start of an important process of disassociation, by which I mean that it starts to implant the understanding that the way you 'land' or are experienced by people can be a distortion of the true you – maybe because you're self-conscious, unaware or fearful, or maybe because you're simply at this stage lacking the tools of the **You brand** craft. Understanding that no one's pointing a finger at you helps to free you up from defensiveness and self-consciousness. And writing down your answers and observations helps acknowledge the need and takes us on the first step from unconscious incompetence to conscious incompetence, which is the start of any learning process.

In order to bridge this 'perception gap', it's not so much having a personality (because we all do!), but the ability to project that personality, that really counts. And doing it in a way that is authentic and congruent, with no sense of insincerity. This starts the moment you enter the room; you don't have the luxury of being able to 'warm up' to it. We can put people in a box the moment we set eyes on them, perhaps before they've even spoken, often because of some conscious or unconscious association we make between them and a past experience or belief system (e.g. are they 'one of us'?). This can work at a very micro level. If someone has a limp handshake we may identify that as weakness, insincerity or being non-committal; or if they're wearing an item of clothing that we associate with a certain type of person or behaviour, then this could predispose us towards them in a certain way.

 Think about the last time this happened to you, or you 'did it' to someone else. What drove it, and what were the consequences of it? How did you feel and how did you deal with it? How long did it take to put right? It's a revealing exercise, one worth trying.

In order to communicate ourselves truthfully and effectively, it's important to be aware of this phenomenon and to work hard to ensure that people's perception of us is aligned with who we really are.

SUMMARY CHAPTER 2

• The way people see us can define who we are: perception is reality.

• How we see ourselves and the way other people perceive us can be hugely different: there's a 'perception gap'.

• If you don't bridge the gap, you're open to interpretation and have no reliable control over the impression you make on people.

• The way people experience you is likely to impact on how they feel about themselves – with significant consequences for your influence and likeability.

Things to work on
If you haven't already, spend a few minutes completing your Personal Profile form. Give it real thought; it's an important start in the process of bridging the perception gap.

CHAPTER 3

You Brand and The Paradox: Looking Natural Doesn't Feel Natural

'Be yourself. Everyone else is taken.'
Oscar Wilde

You brand is the ability to communicate to other people who
you are and what you stand for at all levels with courage and
confidence, whatever type of situation you're in. It has two main
components: character, what makes you who you are – that's 'You'
– and the ability to project and communicate that 'You' whatever
situation you're in – that's 'brand'. **You brand**. It's being able to
appear real, normal, natural and genuine – warts 'n' all – wherever
you are. (You don't have to have warts to benefit from this book!
The expression is attributed to Oliver Cromwell's instruction to
the artist Sir Peter Lely when he was having his portrait painted.
It has come to mean 'the whole thing, without hiding or
embellishing anything'.)

You achieve your **You brand** by mastering *the craft of performing
yourself*. The craft is based on a paradox, which is this: in order to
appear real, natural, normal and engaging wherever you go, you
need to be able to 'perform yourself' – which of course doesn't *feel*
real or natural, and certainly not normal, at least not to begin with!

As we all know to our cost, we don't always feel in control of how
we're coming across. The arena or situation we find ourselves in
may be making us nervous, anxious or overexcited. Or we might
simply be unaware of the impression we're making on people.
Or else we're acutely aware, but don't know what to do about it.
This is why people often hide their true selves by taking on a
protective persona that can act as a buffer to the world. And it's
why you so often hear remarks like 'I just don't get it – s/he's so
different when you meet them down the pub,' or 'If I "act" somebody
else I do much better.'

Professor Catherine Loveday, a neuropsychologist at the University of Westminster, says that 'one of the most stressful things you can do to a human is to ask them to speak or perform in front of a group. It's what we use in labs to make people stressed.' Prof. Loveday found that live performance can produce in musicians levels of the stress hormone cortisol akin to those experienced by a skydiver throwing themselves out of a plane! The effects of performing in front of (or amongst) people should not be underestimated...

But it's not enough just to be able to bridge the perception gap in certain situations and not others. We have to operate and communicate in many different arenas: making friends in the playground or at university, going for our first job or that big opportunity, auditioning or interviewing, presenting to a small group or a large conference, pitching to a new prospective client on Zoom, selling an idea in the boardroom, leading or being part of a team, day-to-day interactions with colleagues, mingling and networking with strangers at drinks parties or other social events, those challenging conversations where your anxiety is closing you down and you just want to hide...

The old mantra 'people buy people' suggests that, if we are to be 'bought' (or believed, followed, listened to, liked) we need to perform consistently across all these different situations. If we appear natural, confident and engaging in one, yet indifferent, cold and aloof in another, then we will confuse people: they won't know quite what they're buying; so we probably won't close the deal, develop the relationship, be heard at senior level, or be remembered as we would wish – if we're remembered at all.
I often ask my clients whether they think they pass what I call the 'Marmite test'. What are the qualities of this iconic brand? Well...

• It is always recognisable.
• You have a relationship with it.
• It is consistent.
• It is reliable.
• It is special, unique.
• It is trustworthy.
• It is authentic – always.

That last point – authenticity – is very important. Marmite's famous slogan – 'You either love it or hate it' – applies to people too (I've been likened to Marmite myself!), and is something to bear in mind when working on your **You brand**. The simple fact, for any brand, is that some people like it, some do not. The worst thing a brand can do is to compromise its values in an attempt to broaden its appeal; it will just lose the things that make it special, and risk alienating everyone.

A good example of an established brand losing sight of its core market is that of one of Britain's longest-established high street retailers. It's where my mum used to go to buy high-quality, reasonably priced clothes. The shop was always consistent and reliable, an instinctive choice for staple items like blouses, skirts, cardigans and jumpers. But then they tried to reinvent themselves, and it seems to me they've been struggling with an identity crisis ever since: they don't know who they are – are they a cool brand, a traditional brand, young or old...? In the process they've alienated their core market and have never really regained it. My mum certainly never forgave them!

It's the same with people. A personal brand is bound by many of the same rules as a commercial brand; and authenticity, being true to yourself, is key. If we over-accommodate to fit in, to be accepted and liked – if in other words we feel 'It's not OK to be me' – it won't have the desired outcome. And we often don't realise this till it's too late, and we wish we'd been more assertive and true to ourselves. As you read on, I hope you'll see this book as a celebration of your uniqueness, that there's no-one else like you in the world.

In fact, paradoxically, our uniqueness is the one thing we all have in common! As Bill Bryson observes in his fascinating book *The Body: a Guide for Occupants*, we are all very different despite being genetically almost identical. Each person's DNA differs from another's in three to four million places; this is proportionally tiny - about 0.1% of our DNA - but enough to make a huge difference between us.

Equally, if we are inconsistent in the way we come over in different situations – not out of any conscious choice, but because of unawareness or the way we feel in the moment – this too can compromise our brand. People will just find us confusing; they won't ever be sure what's real and what isn't. This takes away from our likeability and influence; if people's feeling about us keeps changing because we are never the same person twice, their relationship with us will be undermined because its whole identity will become flaky.

'And the moral of that is—'Be what you would seem to be'—or, if you'd like it put more simply—'Never imagine yourself not to be otherwise than what it might appear to others that what you were or might have been was not otherwise than what you had been would have appeared to them to be otherwise.'
Lewis Carroll: *Alice Through the Looking Glass*

Authenticity, because of the consistency and credibility it brings, is central to many of life's major important roles: leadership, career, relationships, marriage, parenthood – and, most important, our relationship with ourselves. Being aware of who we are and being true to that has a profound and positive effect on how we feel about ourselves and, in my experience, on where we get to in life. But it can be tough to do this! It means that we have to stand by what we believe, and take the consequences, one of which is that not everyone will like us. But 'liking' may be replaced by something just as powerful and valuable: being visibly true to ourselves gives other people permission to be the same – which can have a dramatically cathartic effect on relationships and social and organisational cultures – and even if they don't like us they will probably respect and value us for who we are.

 Years ago I met ex-Prime Minister Maggie Thatcher at a fundraiser in Mayfair. I remember being asked if I'd like to be introduced, and before I knew it I was thrust in front of Maggie, all in grey with a grey handbag. 'And who are you, dear?' she asked, fixing me with piercing blue eyes. I was struggling to know what to say, as I wasn't a Tory supporter, so I blurted out, 'Oh I did a series called *The Brothers*.' 'Oh yes,' she replied, 'one of my absolute favourites.' Encouraged by this, I went on to explain about my business, and the fact that it was she – a woman – who had given me (and many other women) the confidence and permission to start up a business on my own and buy a house. 'So glad to have been of service, dear!' she said. Although our politics were very different and I didn't subscribe to much of what she stood for, I always knew she believed utterly in it and that she was entirely authentic, and so I believed in her, if not in what she did. She was a very powerful brand, one that commanded respect.

In order to appear real, natural, normal and engaging wherever you go, you have to 'perform' yourself – which doesn't feel real or natural initially.

What Determines Likeability?

Karen Keller, a hugely experienced clinical psychologist, piloted her Influence Indicator (KII) on me. I completed a rigorous questionnaire and scored well on most of the influence traits, but relatively low on 'likeability'. Feeling rather insecure, I asked Karen for more context, and she gave me this response: 'If you are a functional adult and are open, clear, direct and articulate wherever you are, you will be in a minority of 30%. 70% of the people around you will not be this way, so they may well not like you; because likeability is about how you impact on others and how consequently they feel about themselves in your company.' That made me realise that I had a choice: I could try to be more likeable by not being myself and fitting more around other people's needs, or I could be myself but more empathic to their needs – **which in turn could up my likeability score!**

At this point I'd like to introduce two hypothetical characters, Alex and Joe, who I'll call on from time to time to help me illustrate certain points, and what happens when someone has a strong **You brand** – and when they don't.

Alex is such an intelligent, relaxed and engaging person to talk to over coffee/drinks/down the pub; but I saw her giving an important presentation of the company's new product the other day and I just didn't recognise her as the Alex I know! Joe, on the other hand, is difficult to communicate with on a one-to-one basis. I always leave feeling I haven't really got what I need; I find him hard to read and rather aloof, so I don't understand where he's coming from and don't feel able to approach him. But I saw him giving a keynote speech at a symposium and he seemed much more effective:

he was more comfortable and in control, and I felt I'd got to know him more in those fifteen minutes than in all the conversations I've ever had with him.

Sound familiar? Well, like many people, neither Alex nor Joe has a brand. They are inconsistent and don't have the skill or awareness to be any different. They fall foul of the paradox that to appear real, natural, normal and engaging you have to perform yourself. Your job is to understand this paradox, work with it and use it to your advantage, so that you are able to look and sound normal, to project a recognisable, natural personality *in every situation you are in*. We are often very aware of the need to do this when we find ourselves in uncomfortable arenas; but it's important to carry this same awareness into familiar situations as well, where our tendency may be to think that we don't have to make any effort ('I'm too important to be here really, so I can do what I like'; or 'I'm not important enough to be here, so no-one will expect me to say anything or make any impression at all'). Never forget: you are always 'on', even in those sorts of situations. When you know how and have the right awareness, you'll be able to take yourself anywhere.

 Fight, Flight or Freeze

The evolutionary process has equipped us with three instinctive responses to fear: fight, flight and freeze. All of these are ways of channelling the energy rush we experience when we feel threatened. This is a prehistoric human instinct that has been programmed into us for thousands of years, and is caused by adrenaline hitting the amygdala, located deep inside the brain. It is this that directs our instinctive behaviour: for example, whether we decide to move towards food or away from danger.

Now, this all worked fine back in the day when we humans were hunting a mammoth to take back to the cave, but translating it into the modern world isn't always straightforward. For example, if we're talking to someone and we really bottle it, we could in theory run out of the room (flight), but we would know that it would be seen as a little weird and we probably wouldn't be invited again, even though running would have been considered perfectly reasonable behaviour in our prehistoric past if we were being chased by some angry beast. So instead we can either freeze – stand there tongue-tied and going red in the face – or fight.

By 'fight' I don't mean hitting people! I mean staying in the room and engaging with the situation we find ourselves in, whether it's a meeting, presentation or some other form of interaction. How successful we are at fighting in the modern world will depend on our level of awareness and ability to manage these situations. If our awareness or ability is relatively undeveloped, we can just struggle on, attempting to make conversation, even though we're finding it really difficult and thinking that we'd much rather be somewhere else (and so probably would the other person!).

Or, we could use our performance skills to harness our fear and appear real and natural. The fear never really goes away; it's always there in some form. Even the most experienced actor feels nerves before they go on; in fact, their performance would suffer if they *didn't* have these feelings. What they do though is to release the fear and use it as fuel for the fight.

 In this book you'll learn how to channel your fear into expression, rather than trying to overcome it by repressing it. This will release a huge amount of the power inside you, which will drive and fuel your performance of you.

When I was fourteen years old I was entered for my Grade 4 piano exam. I'd been having lessons since I was nine; every Sunday I'd reluctantly set off on the train to be taught by two eccentric elderly ladies who were straight out of Agatha Christie, in their beautiful seventeenth-century house full of antiques, worn carpets and dappled sun. The garden was my favourite place, and that and the tomato juice at half-time were the only things that kept me going back! I hated practising and being made to stay in line for a whole hour.

Come the day of my exam I knew that I hadn't done enough work. I was anxious and scared, but determined to go through with it; after all, it would only be me in a small room with my teacher and a judge, wouldn't it? Imagine my horror, then, when I realised I'd be playing in front of a packed hall on a stage with an isolated piano in the middle of it! I sat and waited my turn, growing more stressed by the minute as I heard clever kids playing well. Then it was my turn. I took my place on the stool, acutely aware of the expectation of the audience, of my parents, my teachers... I lifted my hands to start my piece and... nothing! I couldn't move. I had completely frozen.

I have never forgotten the shame, the humiliation, the anger at myself – for not practising and for not preparing properly for that space, for the 'Where'.

But something happened to me a few years later that made me see that I could have escaped from that state of 'freeze' if I'd had the skills to 'fight'.

Aged eighteen, I auditioned for the Royal Central School of Dramatic Art. Before my audition, I was sent some pieces to learn: some Shakespeare and a modern piece. With the help of a fellow drama student (now a well-known actor), I learned and rehearsed the parts thoroughly – the burning shame and fear of my piano experience were still etched in my memory! I practised and practised until I was sure I had everything right.

The big day came and up I went, small and slight, with short blond hair, in jeans and a jacket, to the Embassy Theatre in Swiss Cottage. I'd got my audition place by the skin of my teeth (having applied late), and competition was intense for the two remaining places for that year's intake.

Once again I found myself sitting in the wings, listening to the words and performances of the young hopefuls before me in the queue. But hang on a minute! Those words... they weren't the words I recognised! It was Shakespeare all right – but it was Ophelia and Helena, and the parts I'd been given for the audition were Bottom from *A Midsummer Night's Dream* and Angelo from *Measure for Measure*. 'Excuse me,' I whispered to the stage manager, who was sitting with me in the wings, 'but I seem to have men's parts.' Suppressing a laugh, he duly walked onto the stage and announced: 'Here is Julia, and she has something to tell you.'

By now I was feeling something approaching terror, and it could once again easily have put me into that state of 'freeze', or made me 'flee' – run for my life. But it didn't – I fought back. I walked on stage and told them I had male parts. There were stifled chortles, then a voice from the blackness of the stalls: 'OK, darling, give us your Bottom!' So I went for it. I knew the part backwards (so to speak!) and I was determined to do well – never again was I going to freeze! And I was awarded one of the only two places; I think mainly because I was different, stood out and was very memorable. So whether you flee or freeze in fear, or step forward in confidence, really can change the course of your life.

'Fear generates in you a huge energy. You can use it.
When I feel that mounting fear, I think,
"Oh yes, there it is!" It's like petrol.'
Dame Judi Dench

 You Want To Be Good?
It's Your Choice!
There is strong evidence from the world of neuroscientific research that the things we are 'good at' in life are not determined initially by any hard-wiring in our brain, but rather by what we choose to focus on. We are born with twice as many synapses (the structures that convey signals between our neurons) as we need so as to accommodate every eventuality, every permutation of neural connection that may be required as a result of our actions, thoughts and responses as we pick our way through life; by our late teens this number has been pared down to a stable level, according to what we actually use. Whether we're aware of it or not, we choose the

'Fear generates
in you a huge energy.
You can use it.
It's like petrol.'

Dame Judi Dench

experiences we want to pursue and devote time to them; we practise them, and this is what forms the links in our brain, through a process called myelination – a fatty coating that improves the efficiency of the synapses and helps define the neural pathways in our brain. Myelination is completely dependent on practice.

What has this to do with fight, flight or freeze? Well, earlier on I said the evolutionary process had equipped us with fight, flight and freeze as responses to fear – and the thing about these responses is that they are a choice. You can learn, through practice, to stay and fight, as I did with my Bottom, rather than freezing like me at my piano exam. So the next time you're faced with a situation where you could fight, flee or freeze, remember: the only thing stopping you from doing anything is not your brain – it's you. The choice is entirely yours.

We're going to learn about how communication really works and then you will be able to practise it. Focusing in this way will move you from a place of vague awareness to consciousness; and consciousness – combined with knowing what to do – will give you choice. This will change how you respond to situations, grow your confidence and ability and open up a whole world of new possibilities. How to do this is what we'll start to explore in the next chapter.

SUMMARY CHAPTER 3

• A **You brand** comes from bridging the perception gap: from creating alignment between how other people perceive you with how you see yourself.

• You only have a recognisable personal brand – a **You brand** – if you can bridge the perception gap in all arenas, i.e. you can project your personality, wherever you are.

• **You brand** is based on a paradox: in order to appear real and natural you have to 'perform yourself'; performing yourself doesn't feel real or natural (at least not at first) which is why most people don't do it.

• Certain arenas may make us feel uncomfortable and distort the way we come across, leaving us open to interpretation and not in control of the way other people perceive us.

• You can channel your fight, flight or freeze instinct into expression. Your nerves become your fuel, your friend not your enemy. This will give you great power and equip you to 'fight' effectively in the modern world.

• **You brand** isn't about being liked by everyone, but about being respected for who you are. **You brand** is crucial to success in many of life's most important roles.

• Becoming 'good at' personal communication – or anything else – is a choice you make.

• Awareness brings choice; choice brings confidence.

Things to work on
Think about people in whose company you feel you behave differently from the way you normally are. Reflect on why it is that you change the way you behave when you're with them, and whether this actually creates a good relationship between you. Continue to use your You brand diary or notebook – paper or electronic – to record your thoughts.

CHAPTER 4

Amateur and Professional Communication

'A professional is a man who can do his job when he doesn't feel like it; an amateur is one who can't when he does feel like it.'
James Agate

Communication is a whole person experience. This means joining up the dots between our head, heart and body: intellectual (our thoughts, the framework), emotional (the feeling) and physical (the body). These are our tools of self-expression, and we'll be exploring how we bring them into harmony and alignment so they can do the complicated job of communicating and projecting you at your best, and being able to do this at all times by channelling your feelings – even what seem like negative ones – into positive and productive fuel.

How we look and how we sound has a massive impact on how people feel about us and react to us. This isn't about whether we're thin or round, tall or short, soprano or bass, male or female, black, white or brown. It's about projecting the unique person we are congruently and authentically. This is where personal communication starts, for all of us, and so is naturally a main focus of this book. In order to explore this we first need to get some material to work with. And the material in this book is you. So let's get *you* on camera!

 First piece to camera
Using a video or phone camera – on a tripod, propped up against some books, whatever works – stand (don't sit!) in your preferred space (workspace, bedroom or garden, maybe). Make sure you're on your own and won't be disturbed – it's important that you don't have any audience, and that you just speak to an inanimate object: the camera.

Stand at least ten feet from the camera, and speak direct to it for two minutes or so about you and your job or occupation. If you don't have one, talk about what you want to do. This will be a subject you know well and so it shouldn't need too much thinking about. The important thing is to do it as you would normally. Think of it as the kind of quick summary introduction to yourself that you would give when meeting someone for the first time. Just do what you normally do in these 'introductory' situations, and don't worry if you feel a bit inhibited to start with; just keep going and it will get easier.

Make a note immediately afterwards of how you felt while you were doing it (but don't watch it back – not just yet).

'Just do what I normally do?' Ah, but that's the catch, isn't it? It doesn't feel *normal* in the least, does it? No, of course it doesn't.

Let me give you some clarity. The space between you and the camera is where your feeling of exposure kicks in: 'I am being judged', 'I am vulnerable', 'I must do it well' and so on. It's the same feeling we get when we feel exposed in any way, when we feel like the focus of attention, as if the spotlight is on us. That feeling will put us quite naturally into fight, flight or – horror of horrors – freeze mode. Now here's the (kind of) reassuring bit: that feeling *never* goes away, because it's there for a very important purpose: it gets us ready to deal with the situation. It's the same mechanism we've used for thousands of years to survive when faced with our enemies, as we saw in the last chapter. So how do we use this feeling, rather than letting it distort and undermine us? What happens to us if 'flight' or 'freeze' aren't an option? What does 'fighting' look like?

With anything that is productive but initially scary, we eventually stop simply 'coping' and learn through practice to manage and *use* the fearful feelings we may have from time to time to work for us. Think back to when you learned to ride a bike – remember the fear all the times you wobbled and fell, but then the joy as you pedalled off for the first time unaided and free, leaving your proud parent (or whoever) behind? The fear and nerves tend to recede with practice and experience, but whenever you *do* feel nervous just see that feeling as fuel, and use it, don't try to squash it or repress it. Even seasoned performers still get nervous before they go on – in fact many of them feel it's an essential part of performing well.

Done your filming? Great! What you have done is create the raw material for analysis, and by the time you look back at your recording you'll be looking at it through a more detached and accurate lens than your subjective feelings will allow just at the moment.

 Sit down, make yourself comfortable and close your eyes. Imagine that you have an important situation, presentation, meeting or conversation coming up, or that you've just had one, and that you prepared for it in your normal fashion (whether that was for weeks, hours or minutes before) and you feel confident and reasonably comfortable about the content and the people you are doing it for – done that? Now mentally walk out of that place, telling yourself that you feel dissatisfied with how it went or that you have a feeling that you and your message did not land. Connect to the feeling. Then open your eyes.

You probably don't feel good about yourself or that (imagined) situation. Something was missing in what you did, in the way you put yourself over. What is it, do you think? A clue: without the missing ingredient you might be better off emailing or texting or writing your message. Ask yourself: why were you there in person? Make a short list of what might have been missing. You'll probably come up with very good stuff like:

- Enthusiasm
- Passion
- Sense, clarity
- Confidence
- Preparation

Now, of course all of these things are important, but what we're really looking for is a very basic and physical element that ultimately supports all of the necessary ingredients and makes them manifest, in much the same way that the heat of the oven makes all the ingredients of a cake work and brings them all together.

 Close your eyes again, and imagine that it's your birthday and that the car of your dreams has been delivered to your door. You sit in it and it looks and feels perfect; the leather smells new and wonderful. You put the key in the ignition, the engine turns over... but it doesn't fire. Why not? What's missing?

'Petrol!' you say. Spot on, well done! But what is our petrol, our fuel? What brings us to life, makes it all work, brings our head, heart and body together...?

ENERGY!

Energy is that vital ingredient. It's so fundamental to the craft of professional communication that we'll be exploring it in depth.

First let's look at what gives us energy and what takes it away, what gets us out of bed in the morning – or what makes us want to pull the duvet over our head.

 In your **You brand** diary, write two columns, as below, and populate both columns with as many points as you can think of.

What gives me energy   **and what takes it away**

_____   _____

_____   _____

_____   _____

_____   _____

_____   _____

_____   _____

When you've got a good list of both positives and negatives, start thinking about where your energy comes from mainly and, conversely, what situations, feelings, people and things you find negative and a drain on your energy. This will begin to paint a picture of how you respond to external pressures and stimuli, and the consequent feeling of energy being given or sapped away.

To give you an idea of the sort of thing I mean, and to help get you started, here are some possibilities:

What gives me energy	and what takes it away
people	frustration
challenge	anxiety (describe)
sleep	impatience
a project or task (what?)	intolerance
fear	boredom
being in a team	being on my own/too many people
approval/recognition (which?)	noise/quiet

Now look at your list. What do all the things you've written down have in common? They are all *subjective*. The energy they give us (or take away) is based on how we *feel* about what comes at us from the outside world. It's a fluctuating, reactive energy. In the world of professional performance this is called amateur energy, because it is 'hit and miss'. Using amateur energy will leave us open to interpretation; without a reliable source of energy to sustain us we have little control over what we look like, how we sound and consequently how people read us and react to us. Imagine that beautiful car from the birthday scenario earlier kangaroo-hopping along because a fuel line is blocked. What does that look like and feel like?

Let's look in more depth at how amateur energy works. Imagine that all the positives from the left-hand column are in play, and you are going again into the situation that I asked you to picture earlier: that important presentation, meeting or conversation. You feel good. You are energised, confident and keen to communicate, if a little nervous perhaps – but that's normal. You start, and everything is going well, until a series of occurrences invades your consciousness: you see someone looking at their watch, a mobile phone goes off, someone gets up and walks out, your mind jumps into the future ('What do I want to say?') or the past ('What did I just say?'), builders outside start banging... You hear your own voice droning on. You start to lose your way and your confidence. This is the 'Downward Drift'.

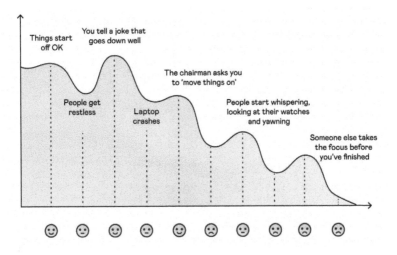

Gradually your energy is sapped, both by what is going on around you and because of your emotional reaction to it. You lose control and can no longer hold your audience in the suspended state that is necessary to keep them focused, engaged and listening.

Look at the graph above. In the peaks, how do you think the audience feels? They have smiling faces, so yes, they are 'connected'. Imagine there are wires running between you and the audience, with a plug on one end and a socket on the other, connecting you with every individual in the audience, whether that's three people or 500.

> *'You take a plug and put it in a socket, and that's what the theatre is – it lights up right away. You speak, and they respond immediately.'*
> Chita Rivera

'You take a plug and put it in a socket, and that's what the theatre is – it lights up right away. You speak, and they respond immediately.'

Chita Rivera

When you're plugged in and switched on they are engaged; there is a live, powerful current passing between you. But when you look at the troughs you see frowning, confused faces. The plug has been pulled out, they are disconnected. How are they feeling now, do you think? And what are they thinking?

Think of the last presentation you were at, or a meeting or conversation you were in. Did you switch off at any point? If so, what was it that triggered your disconnect? And what thoughts did you have?

The audience – or other people in the meeting/conversation – being disconnected or unplugged means that they start to come back to their reality and have the time and space for their thoughts to wander – in other words, they go into their heads. They lose the vital focus that is needed to suspend the reality of the everyday, and questions start to intrude: 'What does s/he mean?'; 'Why am I here?'; 'They haven't prepared'; 'They don't know what they're talking about'; 'I have another meeting to go to'; 'What a boring subject!'; 'I don't understand'; 'What *is* s/he wearing?'; 'I really resent this waste of my time'. And at the end of it, what's the very last thing you want? What's the worst that people can think, the worst feeling they can have about you? Pity.

Amateur energy, then, is hit and miss, inconsistent and unreliable; what we need instead is a more consistent and secure level of energy. We need a ***professional energy*** – one that lifts us out of those subjective feelings that can sabotage us so badly. A safe place. Professional energy is the magic ingredient I promised you at the start of the book. We'll be working with it a lot from now on.

First, though, let's determine what that word 'professional' means. What does a professional approach to anything require? How does it differ from the amateur approach?

At a basic level, **a professional approach is defined as reliably and consistently producing a product or service for which we get paid** – which the amateur doesn't have to do.

Imagine a scale of performance excellence going from 0% to 100%.

At a certain level on this scale is the entry point into professionalism, where amateurism ends and performance makes a step-change that transforms it into a new realm of sustained, consistent, high quality. **It's important to note that there is no**

100%

0%

link, no meeting point, between amateur and professional performance: moving from one to the other is not progressing along a continuum, but rather making a quantum leap into a completely different mindset and way of performing.

Where do you think this dividing line between amateurism and professionalism is? My response to this isn't hugely scientific, but is based on intuition and years of observation – both of which tell me that 50% is too low, because it's not high enough to sustain 'best practice', and 100% is too high, because it isn't sustainable and produces a narrowness of vision. It is rightly said that only an average person is always at their best. I have always seen the professional level as being 70%. It's where 'A' grades in exams usually kick in. It's where, when I was involved in putting on shows in the professional theatre, we typically had consensus about everyone's commitment level. 70% buys you entry into the professional 'club'. You hit 100% when you want to, have to or need to, but you never drop below 70% – or you're out of the club. The zone between 70% and 100%, then, is the professional zone, the performance zone, the place where creativity can happen. You have to inhabit this zone at all times if you are doing a professional job, but you must stay flexible within it.

100%   Professional: 'The Zone'

70% _____

                        Amateur

0%

The Dangers of Driving Slowly

I don't watch it regularly, but a few years ago I caught part of an episode of *Top Gear* in which Richard Hammond was attempting to drive a Formula 1 racing car (a Renault I think it was) round the Silverstone circuit. Quite a challenge as it turned out! His instinct told him that it would be safer to drive slowly to start with, until he'd got the hang of it; but he found that at slow speeds the car was uncontrollable. He observed: 'I'm going as fast as I feel I can, but it's not fast enough to keep heat in the tyres, which means I've got no grip, let alone any downforce. If I go a bit faster it'll be the same, and I'll crash. The only way is to go a lot faster, then I'll have heat in the tyres, and grip, and I won't crash.' Even though it might have felt terrifying (it certainly looked it!), driving fast from the start was the only safe thing to do.

Professional energy – or 'performance energy', as I shall refer to it from now on – is exactly the same: you *have* to have it to do the job, the job of communicating. You must *never* drop down out of the professional performance zone. You can't 'warm up' to it, you have to be on 70% from the start, otherwise you won't have enough metaphorical heat in your tyres and you'll crash. It may feel risky and counterintuitive to start with, but you'll quickly find it's what keeps you safe. It's what I call a 'riskless risk'.

How does this zone operate? What are the laws that govern it? Here's a useful analogy.

The energy tank

Do you remember those old-fashioned cast-iron header tanks that sat in the loft and ensured you got decent water pressure from all the taps in the house? The water in the tank needed to be kept at a certain level in order to maintain this pressure, so as it drained out it was constantly topped up from the mains supply, with the level regulated by a ballcock.

Imagine that within you there is a tank, an energy tank, that works in a similar way to this water tank. In order to stay in the zone, you have to keep this tank topped up to a minimum level of 70%. The situation and the audience, sitting passively before you, can drain energy from you the whole time and, unless you take positive action, you will quickly drop below this level and out of the performance zone.

Unlike a water tank, you are of course not connected to the mains, and so you – and you alone – are responsible for topping up the level. Luckily, you have a bucket! A bucket of energy that you can chuck into the tank whenever you need to.

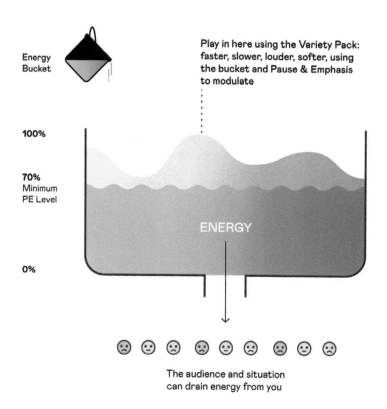

Energy Bucket

Play in here using the Variety Pack: faster, slower, louder, softer, using the bucket and Pause & Emphasis to modulate

100%

70%
Minimum
PE Level

ENERGY

0%

The audience and situation can drain energy from you

The audience is a very thirsty beast and must be managed, so that you can then have a 'conversation' with them (whether or not they actually speak). You do this by getting into the zone and staying in it. Then you will feel their energy by their engagement and attention, which will in turn feed you, and an equal partnership will evolve: you become 'partners in communication'.

What exactly is this performance energy? Where does it come from, what does it look like, what does it sound like? And what's in the energy bucket you use to top it up?

First, a couple of things that performance energy is *not*. It's not about shouting or going over the top, or gesticulating wildly, waving your hands or putting on a manic facial expression (what I call 'energy bollocks'). Performance energy is a level of intensity and definition in your physical and vocal presence that is powerful enough to cut through all the distractions that compete for your audience's attention and engage them with you and what you're saying. Knowing about performance energy will open up a whole new world of awareness inside you. When your performance energy is switched off, you'll feel like a dead weight stuck to the floor. But when it's turned on, it's as if you are bouncing gently on a trampette, primed and ready to take off to whatever level you want.

Being in the professional performance zone gives you access to a set of wonderful tools that simply aren't there in the amateur zone: pace, volume and modulation in your voice; the ability to use your arms and hands in a way that looks natural (because it is) and supports what you are saying – and a host of other things to give flow and definition to what you say. These are part of what I call the Variety Pack, which we'll be exploring soon.

You'll find that, at least to begin with, using performance energy is hard work! It can be physically and emotionally draining, particularly as it's probably something you're not used to using. But it gets easier with practice.

But for now, I want to introduce you to what's in the energy bucket. It contains a fabulous ingredient that allows you to top up your energy level whenever it starts to dip. A very powerful tool that allows all sorts of things to happen, and is essential for the Variety Pack to work properly. It's what allows you to 'change gear', to move off in a new direction, to underline your meaning, to hold and enthral your audience. 'Wow! What can this be?' I hear you ask. What is it that the mysterious thing in the bucket allows you to do?

It allows you to **pause**.

What? Silence?! How terrifying! But a pause isn't the same as stopping talking for a bit. That's just a gap, a hole your audience will drop down, never to be seen again. What makes a pause a pause, and not a gap, is **emphasis**.

> 'The right word may be effective, but no word was ever
> as effective as a rightly timed pause.'
> Mark Twain

The energy that you use to hit a word and give it standout meaning and significance is what buys you the *time* to pause. It is emphasis – the energy of emphasis – that is in the bucket. You have to *earn* the pause in order for it to have real value and meaning. And if you don't use the pause, the emotional meaning of what you're saying will be unclear. The emphasis doesn't have to be on the word that is immediately before the pause, but it does have to be somewhere in the preceding phrase or sentence. You'll know if it's too far away because it won't carry you through the pause.

The Power of Pause and Emphasis – the Dynamic Duo

Emphasis is
the engine that
drives the pause

Between them, pause and emphasis achieve great things. They:
• create variety.

• allow each other to happen, and help you create focus and underline what's important, i.e. which word do you want me to hear and how do you want me to feel about it?

• give you time to breathe! Breathing isn't just about taking in air (important though that is); it can also signal a change of pace, or give a nuance of meaning or emotion.

• give you thinking time (even if you don't need it, the audience will be engaged by seeing you appear to think in the moment – this communicates integrity, thoughtfulness and gravitas).

• give the audience catch-up time – involve them in the conversation and focus them on what's important.

• give you catch-up time: to get a prompt from your pontoons (see Chapter 7) if you need one, or to decide in the moment how you want a word or phrase to land.

• create build, anticipation and excitement.

'Music is the space between the notes.'
Claude Debussy

Emphasis is what connects your emotion to your expression of it. It is your head telling your body what to do. As well as bringing clarity to the meaning of the words, pause and emphasis will help bring clarity to the way you deliver them, to what to do with your face, arms, hands and body. Play around with the following exercise to get a feel for this.

 Take a sentence like 'I never said I'd written you that letter.' Say it through evenly, without emphasising any individual word. Now repeat the line, emphasising the first word: 'I'. Do it again, this time emphasising 'never'... and so on until you've had a go at emphasising every word in the sentence, one at a time. The most obvious thing you'll notice is that there is a significant difference in meaning depending on where you place the emphasis. But you may also notice that you feel almost compelled to take a pause, even if it's just a slight one, after each emphasis. Emphasis doesn't just buy the pause; pause is an almost inevitable consequence of it. And you may also experience this: as you emphasise a word, your hands come into play very naturally, and energy is released into your face. If you're not sure what I mean, practise in front of the mirror and see for yourself.

I know we've covered a lot of ground in this chapter and it's a lot to take in all at once, but these are some of the key concepts we'll be working with, so I wanted to plant the seed early. We'll be looking at all of this in depth, and doing some practical exercises that will launch your energy into the performance zone, in a short while.

So please read on!

SUMMARY CHAPTER 4

• Face-to-face communication is a whole person experience in which head, heart and body need to be engaged.
This is our toolkit.

• How we look and sound has a huge impact on how people feel about us.

• Subjective, amateur energy is unreliable and leaves us vulnerable to 'downward drift'.

• Professional, 'performance' energy is what we need to communicate to a professional level of effectiveness and consistency. It's the 'magic ingredient'.

• Your 'energy tank' needs to be kept at least 70% full at all times. Top it up with an energy bucket of pause and emphasis – this will keep you in the zone and allow you free use of the Variety Pack.

Things to work on
Make sure you've completed all the exercises in the chapter. You may want to spend a bit more time reflecting on what gives you energy and what takes it away, and add anything you think of or become aware of to your list. Watch a TED talk, or someone making a presentation or speaking in a meeting: analyse what they're doing by reference to everything you've learned so far – and rate their performance!

CHAPTER 5

The Drivers of Perception and How to Power Yourself Into the Professional Zone

'Be yourself – more – with skill.'
Rob Goffee, Emeritus Professor, London Business School

Albert Mehrabian, an Armenian psychologist and Professor Emeritus of Psychology at UCLA, did some research into the impact of the various components of verbal communication. The things he discovered can help to give us a whole new perspective on how communication works, and what drives the effect we have on an audience or someone we're in conversation with.

The following exercise is important. It will unlock a door.

 Imagine that this circle, a pie chart, represents 100% of the impact, the first impression, that you can make on another person.

Without giving it too much thought, and being as instinctive as you can – **and before you look at the answer below!** – answer these three questions, giving your answers as percentages.

1. How much of the impact comes from how you *look*? Remember, your visual impact isn't just about what clothes you're wearing; it's about facial expression, your smile, eye contact, body language...
2. How much from how you *sound*?
3. And finally, how much from what you *say*, from the words you use?

Here is the 'Communication Wheel':

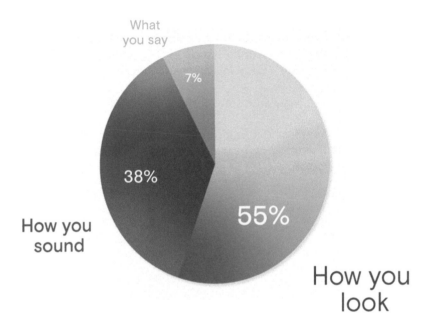

Mehrabian found that if there is incongruence between a person's verbal and non-verbal communication, it is likely that the receiver will trust the predominant form of communication, that is the impact of tone + facial expression/gestures (38% + 55% = 93%), rather than the literal meaning of the words (7%).

Compare this to your circle. What did yours show? Probably that much more trust and impact come from the verbal elements; after all, the rational and logical brain will naturally be thinking, 'Surely *what* we say is the most important element – it's the content, for heaven's sake!'

But Mehrabian's conclusions say otherwise. Getting the three elements of the circle into balance is key; if any one of them comes out of proportion we start to lose our reality and credibility.
The degree of harmony between how we look and sound and the words we use will influence people in how far they understand and accept what we say. As a simple example, try saying in front of the mirror something like, 'There's nothing I like better than going out to a great restaurant with fun people,' with a deadpan face and a dull, lifeless voice. Do you believe the words you're saying? Thought not.

I'm <u>so</u>
excited!

Put another way: if the 93% is working well (if we look and sound authentic and engaging) we are a golden gun, an infallible weapon. But if what we say is a rusty old bullet (superficial, bullshit, disorganised, pointless...), we and our message do not hit the target, do not 'land'. Conversely, if we fire a golden bullet from a rusty old blunderbuss, again, we don't hit the target, our message isn't heard in the way we intend. But if we have a golden gun firing a golden bullet, then wham! We hit the bull's-eye.

Now wouldn't it be great to be able to do that more often?

Let's look at how you can...

Looking at your first performance to camera through the lens of the Communication Wheel

Remember the piece to camera you did in Chapter 4? Let's return to it. Play back the first part of the piece, but without sound: yes, that's right – hit the mute button or turn the volume right down. Focus entirely on how you look. What is your physicality telling us? Are you moving or static? Are you using your arms and hands, or are your hands clasped in front of you or behind your back? Is your face expressive? Are your eyes looking away, down or up? What messages are you getting from the way this person (you) looks? Do you recognise yourself – or don't you? Do you feel you would like to hear what this person is saying? Are you wanting more – or not? Do you like them? Would you trust them?

Now close your eyes and turn the sound up. Listen for just a few seconds, then hit pause. Open your eyes. Based on what you had *seen*, were you expecting what you then *heard*? Did you experience harmony between your vocal impact and your visual one? Or was there a disconnect between the two? Were you getting two different – and consequently confusing – signals? (You probably wouldn't be aware of this if you were watching and listening to someone at the same time, which is what we usually do.)

What you are looking for here is where the energy is: are body and voice in balance, or is there more energy in the body than in the voice or vice versa? For instance, if the voice is clearly audible, with plenty of tone and expression, but the body is still, we will start to notice only the body as its energy is out of harmony with the energy in the voice. And the reverse: if the body has expressive movement and there is vitality in the face, but the voice is a dull monotone, again we will be aware (possibly subconsciously, but aware nonetheless) of a disconnect, a lack of congruence between the *look* and the *sound*.

In either case, the incongruence leaves you '*open to interpretation*', because the disconnected signals are confusing. What your audience comes up with in terms of how they view or judge you may be far from the 'truth' or what you intend – but remember: perception is reality!

As well as the degree of congruence between how someone looks and how they sound, here are some of the things I commonly observe in this first piece to camera.

- Hands: are they connected with and supporting what the person is saying? Are their gestures stiff, minimal or non-existent? Or are their hands flailing all over the place?
- Low vocal energy
- Confusing eye contact: looking up or down, or off to the side
- Not enough light and shade in the voice, and/or a 'tune' to the voice that isn't helpful. A consistent downward inflection (going down at the end of each sentence or phrase) suggests you're running out of energy; consistent rising inflection suggests approval-seeking, an unspoken 'You know what I mean?' (I've heard it described as the 'moronic interrogative'). It can also sound as though you're reeling off a list that has no real importance.
- Too fast, too soft, too loud
- No pause
- Swallowing words
- Um and er
- No 'I' (personal disclosure) to tell us how you feel
- A list (tends to go hand in hand with a 'tune' in the voice)
- Facial expression – smile or lack of, open, warm or not. Smiling too much?
- Head on one side
- Nice persona but a confusing message
- Bleeding energy (when nervous energy is being sat on or repressed, not used properly as fuel). Can include, for example, jiggling backwards and forwards, wandering, grinding a heel, unconnected hand movements, head on one side, rigid posture, leaning on one hip.
- What is the message and am I getting it? (No narrative structure)

Hands

The feeling of being judged, exposed, 'on the spot' – or simply being unaware – can do strange things to us. Basically what happens is that we feel frightened and our adrenaline starts to pump, which is our fuel and signal to either fight or flee. This is all great if we're in physical danger, but if flight is not a viable option – if we're in the middle of a sales pitch, for example – and if we don't know how to fight, what happens? Freeze! But the powerful energy that has now been unleashed inside has to go somewhere, so it 'bleeds'. It dribbles out through our feet, and they start to tap or shuffle with no real purpose, so we look a bit demented or twitchy.

Or through our hands as we scratch, poke a finger into our eye, clasp and clutch, looking like a cross between Uriah Heep and Lady Macbeth endlessly scrubbing her hands clean. Or we simply hide them in our pockets or behind our back – or go over the top and gesticulate wildly and randomly (remember the 'energy bollocks' I mentioned earlier?).

Imagine this. Your hands are simply a conduit for all that stressful nervous energy in your tummy. Pump it up through the hollow tubes of your arms and out through your hands to use as fuel. This will look completely natural, engaged and engaging, to the point people won't even notice. It will also stop you going into freeze; it's part of the modern-day equivalent of 'fight' – using adrenaline and nerves to fuel your body and voice to communicate rather than fuelling your fists to hit someone.

Remember that communication is intellectual, emotional and *physical* – it gets us moving, and we need to move to do it. If your thoughts and feelings are aligned, your body will follow, and support their meaning – but only if you break through your inhibitions and let it.

Vocal energy
When you play your piece back you may well hear your voice as rather monotonous. Understand this: your voice is a recorder as much as it is a speaker. It expresses how you feel, which in turn helps people to understand more clearly what you mean and how we are to feel about what you say (remember: how you sound: 38%). When there is little vitality or *energy* behind the voice, it will come out as a monotone. A bit like a painter with their different oils, your voice offers you a rich palette of colour, but mostly you'll be using black and white, or grey. This undermines clarity and engagement because it is hard to understand and not inspiring to listen to. Try saying to yourself, with as little energy and expression as possible: 'I'm ever so excited about the holiday I'm going on.' What do you believe? The words themselves, or the tone of voice? But when you 'fire up' your voice and give it light and shade, and are committed to what you're saying, everything changes. We'll be working on this when we come on to the Energy Exercises in a short while.

Speed
If you talk too fast you make it difficult for people to 'hook in' to your meaning. When there are no 'beats' in between the words and phrases or sentences, it is very difficult to understand or keep

an emotional connection (try to spot when this happens the next time you listen to the radio or watch TV). All the words start to have equal stress and value, so listeners can make little sense of the intention of the words and their brains have no time to process or keep pace. Nothing 'lands'. There is just too much to deal with, so a listener will turn off; or make a much reduced interpretation, missing the subtleties and nuances, where the true meaning often resides.

Face

As we touched on when looking at the Communication Wheel, 93% of our impact comes from how we look and sound, with how we look being 55% of that. What message is your face conveying? Is it open and friendly or 'hard to read'? Smiling helps you to relax, as well as the people you're talking to. But just like your voice and body language, your facial expression must be congruent and in harmony with what you're saying and how you're saying it.

Who is s/he?

You have to be at the centre of your presentation, talk or conversation or you are not visible. Your audience wants to know about you, or at least about your perspective and individual lens on what you're talking about, and the only way that can happen is if you use personal disclosure to build connection and presence. For example, if you say, 'I find the situation I'm in far more challenging than I ever imagined,' with confidence, we can relate to that and feel we are getting to know you – and we want to know more. But if you talk about 'we' or 'you' or 'one' and never 'I', there is no real ownership and consequently no heart in the communication. It's boring and we switch off. But the 'I' must be a warts 'n' all 'I', confidently showing your vulnerable, insightful self – the real you. When we use 'I' against ourselves – when we reveal our own fears and complexities and demonstrate our human vulnerability – it allows us to go deeper into things, because we're not being in any way accusatory. This is how we relate to each other, by sharing our human experience. We're obliquely inviting other people to examine themselves by examining us. When we open up we bring people in. It's what great comedians, great speakers and good leaders do.

Lists

A repetitive tune to the voice, with each phrase ending in a rising inflection, makes what you're saying sound like a list. In my experience 'listing' is usually unintended and comes from a lack of awareness and little real ownership of what we're saying. But whatever the cause, you might just as well stand there and say, 'What I'm telling you is deadly boring, I wouldn't bother to listen.'

The only message that lands is that this is a chore to be got through, and the only thing anyone's likely to remember is the feeling of relief when you've finished. Sounding like a list will set 'downward drift' in motion practically as soon as you open your mouth. One of the things that will help you avoid listing is *structure* – more on this later...

How do you increase your energy in a way that brings the different elements of the Communication Wheel into alignment? In other words, how do you get performance energy?

Ah, that is the question! And you are going to get to the answer – but you're going to have to do the following exercises to find it. I can't overemphasise the importance of these exercises, so please don't skimp on them! They're a pivotal part of the whole programme. This is the fuel that brings it all together and that will start the evolution of your **You brand** by harnessing the 'Big Three' of personal communication:

• The Intellectual: the structure and the logic – the 'content'
• The Emotional: the meaning and the feelings – the connection
• The Physical: the expressive demonstration of the intellectual and the emotional

You need all three to be aligned, congruent and working in harmony and supported by the right level of energy (almost certainly higher than you normally use). Then an audience can understand and accept you as real and genuine. When this happens, if people still disagree with you or dislike you, they are at least basing their assessment and response to you on a reality, rather than on a version of you that has become distorted in its communication.

Let's get started with the exercises! I recommend you read through the following series of exercises first to familiarise yourself with them before having a go. You may feel inhibited to start with (even though you're alone in a room), but persevere and you'll get into it. *Do please* let yourself go! One important objective of the exercises is for you to experience the gap between how you feel and how you actually look – do the exercises and you'll see what I mean...

THE ENERGY EXERCISES
Step 1
Set up your camera or phone, and sit in a chair about eight feet away (an armless chair with an upright back is best – NOT an armchair or anything that doesn't give you good support). You will record all of these exercises, so it might be worth checking in on your camera occasionally to make sure it's still recording.

Turn on the camera and start to have a conversation with it – but imagine you're talking to me, your coach, Julia. Talk about something you feel strongly about: it could be a hobby, a world view, your family, football. Do this in a very relaxed way for this first part of the exercise; slide down in your chair and imagine you are down the pub with a friend, or in any other environment you find really relaxing. Talk for about five minutes. You may find it helpful to ask yourself a question to get you going, e.g. 'How do I really feel about my work/life/ family/global warming/politics/playing golf/yoga/the rellies?' Let the camera become your friend. It's really rather nice, you might find, to talk to a camera and so run no risk of being interrupted.

Step 2

Sit up in the chair: sit on your sitting bones with your spine straight, pelvis tilted slightly forward, ear over shoulder – imagine there's a thread pulling up from the crown of your head – but stay relaxed, don't stiffen up. Plant your legs about hip distance apart, your feet flat on the floor, hands resting lightly and openly on your thighs or lap. This is called the 'neutral' or 'ready for action' position. It may feel weird to start with, but it will soon transform how you look and feel. Now you are physically taking more active ownership of your space and have more authority.

Keep your hands open and relaxed and bring them up to elbow height, ready to use. Now I want you consciously to use your hands to express and choreograph what you say and how you feel about it. Do not drop them at any time, but bring them to rest, when you need to, at chest height. This may well make you feel very self-conscious about your hands, but try to just do it.

Now talk to the camera about the opposite sex (or about the same sex, depending on where you sit on the LGBTQ spectrum). The emotional narrative here is important for the exercise. Again, talk to the camera as if it were a friend (or me). Start the process by imagining your friend has asked you to talk about men or women. There are many aspects of this subject you could talk about: men/women in the workplace, in your life (mother, father, sister, brother, boss), what you observe in them, how you connect, and so on. Use your hands to physically express and externalise your feelings and meaning. Your hands, as an extension of your meaning, *will* slow you down and make the meaning clearer. This will also support your use of pause and emphasis, the dynamic duo, to give specific meaning to certain key words and phrases. You will now begin to *feel* your physical expression, the words you say and the real feeling behind them start to come together. The impact of this can be sensational.

Step 3

The aim of this stage is to bring projection and performance energy into what you're doing. As you may have realised, this is an evolutionary learning process, and the layers of understanding and practice that go with it will bring clarity and start to create new neural pathways in the brain – but practice is the key.

Ask yourself this question: What can't we do at the same time as perform and communicate really well? The answer is... we can't think, or process. So we need to be very clear about where we are going, but not necessarily how we are going to get there, as we need to be 'in the moment' and 'present' at all times. It's natural to think: 'I must get it all worked out before I speak' or 'I haven't worked it out properly, so I'm trapped into trying to remember and work it out at the same time.' But if you do that, where do you think your focus and consequently your energy will go? Into your head! And when that happens, the energy tank starts to drain, your expressiveness and physicality disappear and you end up coming across as dull and monotonous. It's all too easy to become obsessed with learning everything by heart, and in the process losing all personality and spontaneity – or else not preparing at all and just 'winging it'.

The next part of the exercise shows you a different way: how to have time, how to create real expressive variety and clarity of intention, *in the moment*. First of all you need an empty mind, with no thinking or processing needed, so you can be absolutely present and *not* in your head.

Sit on your sitting bones, upright in your chair, bring your hands to chest height and breathe. And start talking about... butterflies! Say anything you like; you don't need to know anything about butterflies at all. It can be a flight of fancy, stream of consciousness, a load of rubbish – but don't think! Just let it come. Then after about thirty seconds go louder –

still talking about butterflies – louder, bigger – now go right over the top and *shout*, but not with anger, just with vocal power. Now use your arms and hands to choreograph and support what you're saying... keep the energy and volume up... now start to go slower... then slower and quieter. Bring yourself into a slow, quiet, intimate place, speaking almost in a whisper... now freeze! Then from a 'standing start' (but stay sitting down!), hit the accelerator, go from 0 to 60 miles an hour and speed up. Then after a few seconds, **pause**... hold the pause but don't drop your energy or focus... now hit any words you like, at random, with emphasis... go loud on certain words, just as it comes to you naturally, as you continue to talk about butterflies. This should now be becoming quite creative, mad and fun! Let go of your inhibitions and self-consciousness – you're alone in a room after all – and go for it.

Now, listen carefully to this next bit: I want you to start using the **pause**, with **emphasis** – remember the 'tank' model? The energy needed to sustain a pause (and to make it an actual pause with real power, rather than just a lifeless gap) comes from emphasis (remember the dynamic duo).

Give yourself this simple instruction when you're speaking: '1-2-3-lift.' When you've emphasised a word, pause for the count of 1-2-3, then on 'lift' throw a bucket of energy onto the next word. For example:

Wrong way:
'I feel very strongly about this' – all on one note.

Right way:
'I **feel** (with emphasis) 1-2-3 (pause) very **strongly** (lift: bucket of energy) about this.'

or...
'I feel very **strongly** 1-2-3 about **this** (lift).'

There are many different meanings you can give to the same set of words simply by placing pause and emphasis, and tone and pace, differently. But this can only happen when you have performance energy supporting the process – then you have a great deal to play with within the performance zone. This is what I term the '**Variety Pack**': louder/softer, faster/slower, using pause and emphasis to modulate and make the gear shifts that keep your delivery dynamic and give it depth and texture, clarity and emotional meaning.

Now here's one last brilliant tool that will really raise your game and set you apart. It will let you buy much more time 'in the moment', allowing you to stay real and present while giving your brain the time it needs to land meaning and understanding, and for your audience to have time to catch up and take in what you've said or wait in expectation for what's coming next. The tool is **bridging words**, which include:

So...
Therefore...
But...
And...
Now...
Or...

To get the maximum time and impact from the pause, try this. Say the following. Say it all on one note, quickly, with low energy:
'I feel we have a fantastic opportunity, but there's a lot of work to be done.'
Now say and do this:
'I feel we have a fantastic opportunity, 1-2-3 **but** (bridging word and throw your energy bucket) 1-2-3 there's a lot of *work* 1-2-3 to be done.'
Using pause and emphasis, together with bridging words, takes the impact of what you say to a much higher level. And performance energy gives you the space to be quiet, with intent.

Now practise this all through the next part of the exercise, until you feel its power. Remember though, you need probably twice the energy you feel comfortable with for it to work, to get out of your head and into your body and emotion.

Fred
Now I'd like you to tell a story about 'Fred the Butterfly' (or Freda – or both), using all of the Variety Pack: louder/softer, faster/slower, with pause and emphasis to modulate, and always underpinned by a minimum of 70% performance energy. And all from a standing start. Use your arms and hands to reinforce your meaning. And smile! So...

'Once upon a time there was a butterfly called Fred...' 1-2-3 and a bucket of energy as you start the narrative. Stop and start if you have to, but try to keep going. Give your story a beginning, middle and end: after two or three minutes bring it to a conclusion and leave us with a meaningful message or a moral. Let the story take you. You are Fred.

Performance energy will allow your imagination to create something, quite spontaneously, and make it flow, without any conscious editing. The pause will give you time to find the next bit without involving your head and the processing part of your brain.

The three takeaways from the energy exercises are:

1. Being on, and sustaining, a 70% energy level and above is hard physical work! It takes real effort. It feels like a workout. This is the experience of being 'out of your head' and it's self-expression at its most acute. Feel the connection and how it releases your energy and takes away inhibition. But it is done without emotional drive or making any real 'sense'. This is performance energy using your physical and vocal power purely as a means to an end – louder/softer, faster/slower – with pause and emphasis as your guide and modulator – sort of performance by numbers.

2. When you watch yourself back you'll realise that what you felt was 'over the top' and stupid just looks more interesting, has more light and shade, more colour to the tone of your voice, there's more meaning to what you're saying. If you release your brain from the straitjacket of intellectual programming and pre-thought and give it expressive freedom, it will automatically make sense, but you have to release it from inhibition by using the power of performance energy.

3. And the third most important understanding is that it is not *what* you say but *how* you say it (90% of conflicts are caused by tone of voice – think of the last argument you had with your partner, friend, colleague or teenage child!).

The energy exercises are the most important and private part of the work: we have to break out of the comfort zone of hiding our expressive self. Remember, above all, that this isn't about 'getting it right'. The important thing to do in these exercises is to experiment, to try out and practise all the tools and to break out

Being on, and sustaining, a 70% energy level and above is hard physical work! It takes real effort. It feels like a workout.

of any inhibitions you have and let yourself go – and then see what it looks and sounds like when you play it back. I guarantee you'll find that it's very hard to actually go 'over the top', no matter how over the top it may feel when you're doing it. If you practise enough, you'll start to reconcile what it *feels* like to *look* and *sound* the way that works best for you, and eventually this will work its way into your muscle memory so that you'll be able to perform yourself, instinctively, whenever you want. It's one of the greatest gifts in the world. Well worth all the work and pain!

SUMMARY CHAPTER 5

• How we look and sound has a big influence on the way people feel about what we say and how they respond to us.

• Incongruence between how we look, how we sound and what we say means we are not in control of the impact we make.

• Performance energy helps us to achieve congruence.

• The 'Variety Pack' – louder/softer, faster/slower, using hands, vocal energy, facial expression, body language, with pause and emphasis to modulate – will help you stay in the professional performance zone (70%+) and keep your delivery dynamic. This is part of what gives you 'freedom within a framework', which we'll be looking at in the next chapter.

• Using pause and emphasis with bridging words is a powerful tool to buy time and land your message, and connect you and your audience emotionally.

• Staying in the performance zone is hard work.

• What may feel 'over the top' in fact looks real, natural and engaging, and has more colour.

• The power of performance energy releases the brain to work its magic: performance energy supports and catalyses the brain's ability to extemporise and find structure and expression in the moment.

Things to work on
Revisit the energy exercises and play around with them. Keep recording yourself and playing back, and see what works well. Focus on what it *feels* like to look and sound a certain way.

CHAPTER 6

Story and
The Power
of Disclosure

'Human minds yield helplessly to the suction of story. No matter how hard we concentrate, no matter how deep we dig in our heels, we just can't resist the gravity of alternate worlds.'
Jonathan Gottschall: *The Storytelling Animal: How Stories Make Us Human*

Now that we have this fabulous performance energy, we need a structure to channel and direct it – otherwise it can become random and unfocused and gush out all over the place. Also, it is difficult to process information and thoughts at the same time as performing and projecting, so it's invaluable to have a structure that will help us stay on track and on message – but one that is also flexible enough to allow us to extemporise, and to adapt our message to the needs of a specific person or audience. We need something that allows us 'freedom within a framework'.

Happily, just such a framework exists. What's more, we're all familiar with it and have been using it, as a race, for thousands of years. We bring it into our homes in countless ways. We spend huge amounts of money on it. It's no exaggeration to say we couldn't live without it. It's what Jesus used to convey complex religious doctrine to ordinary people. It is the core and anchor that define theatre and make it work. What is it? It's the **story**, of course.

But what exactly is a story? And what makes it so powerful?

You have (hopefully) already experienced for yourself what a natural affinity we have with story. In the energy exercises, when I asked you to talk generally about butterflies, you probably found it much easier to keep speaking if you applied a story structure rather than just coming out with randomly expressed descriptions. And in the 'Fred the Butterfly' exercise, when I asked you specifically to tell a *story* about Fred, even though you had done *no* mental preparation or written anything down, I'll bet you knew where you were going and roughly how you were going to get there *and* – with a bit of prompting – what the message was that you wanted to leave us with. Our affinity with story is so strong that your brain will work it out for you – if you let it and if you give it the right triggers.

The Storywheel
When I first started to use the Storywheel it was simply to help people focus on a structure to enable them to communicate verbally with enthusiasm, energy, belief and freedom. But as I worked with clients using the Storywheel it became clear to me that story offers a complete personal performance framework that is extremely rich and layered.

Story is something we inhabit and that lives within us; if we let it, it can naturally and effortlessly give shape and purpose to our lives in all sorts of ways on top of how we communicate. We develop our personal narrative over time, and this unique journey of experience and observation is a rich source of material we can draw on as we tell the story of ourselves, the things that are important to us and the people and situations we interact with. The fundamental structure of story will keep you safe – or, in other words, keep you clear, authentic and impactful. You will be free to be **you** and to fly like a bird.

The main constituents of Story as incorporated into the Storywheel are Plot, Beginning, Middle and End, Theme, Images and Personal

Disclosure. These components are so interlinked that you can start at any point on the Storywheel. The reason I represent them on a wheel is that a story has to **turn**. It needs **energy** to start turning and keep going, and also a **framework** or structure to keep on track. Let's look at where this energy and structure come from.

Personal disclosure

At the heart of the Storywheel is the storyteller: **you**. How do *you* get connected to your story in order to connect us? To continue the analogy of energy I used when describing 'downward drift' in Chapter 4, the story is like an electrical lead, with one end plugged into you and the other into the audience. The energy of the story has to travel between you, and when the lead's unplugged nothing's happening...

We first need to plug ourselves in, to engage ourselves – this is vital. A reliable way to do this is by using personal disclosure – bringing in an 'I' statement. For example: 'I nearly always regret judging people by their appearance, but it's something I struggle to avoid doing' or 'Every time a friend succeeds, a little something inside me dies' (Gore Vidal, allegedly).

Do this early on (you don't necessarily have to do it right at the very start, but don't leave it too long) to hook us in, then use personal disclosure every so often to centre what you're saying and ground it in personal experience.

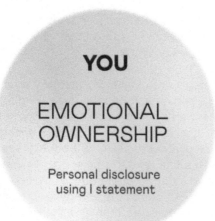

YOU

EMOTIONAL
OWNERSHIP

Personal disclosure
using I statement

Many people find this hard because they think, 'Oh, if I disclose personal things aren't I just going to look weak? Aren't I going to be vulnerable, feel exposed?' What I always say to them is that only confident people use disclosure. Because, as a way of connecting with people, the power and impact of personal disclosure are better than anything in the world. You need to show and share your humanity and humility in order for your listeners to relate to you, from the imperfect human level we all inhabit. You must draw on your own 'inscape' but, crucially, also on shared human experience. This makes you simultaneously both special and real – and a listener will learn something from you and relate to you at the same time (in fact we learn precisely *because* we relate). *You* give *us*, your listener, permission to be ourselves. Think of Prince Harry sharing with the world his mental stress about the death of his mother, or Michelle Obama saying goodbye to her followers. Or think of someone you know who has moved you to tears or made you laugh with stories of their adversity. The specific experience is their own; but the idea of saying goodbye, or of dealing with grief, is understandable to us all.

As an audience, hearing a speaker's humanity in their personal disclosure is how we really understand a message, take it on board for ourselves and relate to it. We feel we're on the same level as the other person, connected with them, and that they're not somehow beyond the reach of us mere mortals (this is why many TED talks are so powerful).

Yes, of course personal disclosure shows vulnerability. But only in the same way that a high-wire act does. When done confidently – this is the key – personal disclosure embodies the same paradox as 'only really strong people express themselves gently' and 'only masters make complexity simple'.

For a speaker, personal disclosure is massively powerful: it releases *emotional energy*, and establishes the underlying **feeling** that runs through what we say. This emotional energy – energy that is expressed, not repressed – is ***performance energy.*** Great performance comes from the ability to both express and control emotion at the same time, and it is performance energy that gives us the intensity and intent to project this knife-edge balance. Emotional energy is our petrol, the energy for ourselves, and with it we can start to energise others, which is otherwise almost impossible to do. How do you do it?

Great performance comes from the ability to both express and control emotion at the same time, and it is performance energy that gives us the intensity and intent to project this knife-edge balance.

How do you do it?

It can be surprisingly difficult to come up with a really effective piece of personal disclosure. Which is why you so often hear people coming out with 'I'm really delighted to be here...' or 'I'd like to share with you...', nearly always delivered in a way that makes it

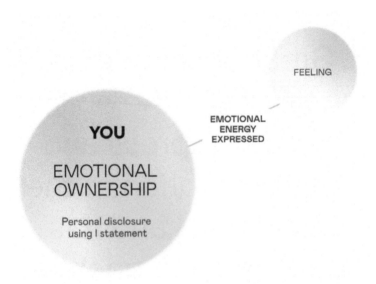

obvious they'd much rather be somewhere else and that they don't really want to share anything. Saying something to shock or provoke – such as 'Talking to you today is not something I want to do at all' or 'I'm terrified that the world as you and I know it is coming to an end' – isn't necessarily helpful either, of course (although either of these openings will certainly get people's attention!). If you try too hard the chances are you'll appear contrived and fake, and you may have the opposite effect from the one you want: if the experience you describe is too rarefied or extreme, people are likely to feel shut out rather than invited in.

If I'm stuck, I find this can help: I ask myself: 'What is it about this subject that I really feel, and that everyone else is likely to be feeling but no one likes to say because they're worried they'll look stupid or be seen as controversial?' So things like 'A lot of modern technology makes me feel stupid' or 'I've often found that not doing things out of fear has given me far more regret than doing things impetuously.' Encouraging people to peer over the cliff edge of their own potential failings, shortcomings, regret or hurt by sharing your own vulnerability is guaranteed to make them receptive to what you have to say. (But only ever use what's true! If you fake it, it simply won't work.)

Here's an example of what I mean:

In 2008 I was in a tent in Kenya, having my first close contact with the wild animals of the Masai Mara, when my mobile bleeped and a message appeared on the screen that said ,'OK, that time has come, it's your turn. You are being honoured by the Dyslexia Association for your services to the theatre and the world of business.'

Wow! I felt at that moment like when I was ten years old and was made vice-captain of Green Team and awarded a special badge, which I treasured.

When it came to accepting my award on the stage in the Dorchester Hotel in front of a roomful of sophisticated, successful and somewhat intimidating people from all walks of life, I knew I had to speak meaningfully but simply to reach them in the very short time I'd been given. So I told them

how I felt in that tent, and why. How the power of that moment in the tent took me right back to a feeling and a place: in the darkness of the bedroom I shared with my two sisters, holding my little green badge, looking at it sitting in my hand and feeling recognised. Almost nothing I had done before or since, until that moment in the tent, came close.

I had always been a misfit. We moved homes seven times before I was seven years old, and I went to a string of awful, freezing-cold village schools where I was always the outsider, the newbie. I was never chosen to be part of a team in the playground or on the sports field. I always had to push for things and, as a result, stand out – in a vulnerable, uncomfortable, exposed way. I don't have a single memory of joy from this time, just memories of never fitting in with the village kids, being shut out, alone in the playground. So this badge, at last, gave me a sense that despite my struggle I was worth something. I was given just ninety seconds to speak, but putting it together in this way meant that the audience was able to relate to it, feel it and remember it.

It would have been all too easy to resort to one of the usual acceptance speech platitudes, such as 'I'm delighted to be here this evening', or 'I'm honoured to receive this award.' But instead I delved deep into my true feelings about the award and exactly what it represented for me. I opened with: 'For most of my life I've felt like an outsider, different.' This piece of disclosure resonated strongly with the audience, many of whom had also struggled for most of their lives with dyslexia.

This speech brought home to me one of the real benefits of using personal disclosure, one we've already touched on with Prince Harry and Michelle Obama: disclosure invariably lives within an actual experience that you've had, so it comes ready-wrapped in a story that has existing drama, characters, images and truthfulness; in other words, a clear narrative flow. So my speech 'wrote' itself (though I didn't actually write it down – I didn't have to), and practically told itself. That's because inhabiting and telling a story is a much easier way of communicating and remembering – there is hardly any need for notes or reminders, no need to process it for yourself or for your audience. You always know where you're going and you can take people with you, easily and fluently. A favourite expression I use with clients is 'Be more of yourself – with skill.' Disclosure is a potent part of that skill.

Don't get me wrong. I didn't do my speech entirely off the cuff. I planned it and practised it out loud, and I did have a few carefully chosen pontoons to keep me on track. You'll be learning all about pontoons in the next chapter.

Some key elements of personal disclosure

• To be effective, disclosure mustn't be formulaic: as well as being appropriate to the specific audience, it needs to be natural, genuine and truly personal, and come from a place of emotional connection and self-awareness. A discipline I follow when distilling my thoughts and feelings about any subject is to ask myself (and really push until I get there!): 'What would be my one piece of personal disclosure about this?' As well as producing something that audiences will love, the creative rigour of this process has the added advantage that it will likely move your thoughts and feelings – and your communication of them – to a whole new level.

• The delivery of your disclosure has to be confident. If it's diffident, or over the top, then your audience will read this (subconsciously at least) as a warning to be wary, rather than as a warm invitation to join with you in a shared experience and that it's safe to do so. The tone of your voice is crucial in making personal disclosure work. If you make an 'I' statement in an under-energised, negative or critical voice, as a listener I might feel negatively about it and, by extension, about you. Whereas if you say it confidently, I'm likely to feel able to own up to having felt similarly and so be able to relate to you.

• In my experience, the type of personal disclosure that works the best tends towards the introspective and the challenging, rather than optimistic and upbeat. I don't think this is necessarily to do with the perversity of human nature (though this may come into it); it's more to do with how story works, and what grabs our attention at an instinctive level. It's about setting up a challenge or an obstacle, something that will give what we say next real traction, and introduce suspense and drama into our story (we'll look at this more closely when we come to examine plot and structure, other key ingredients of story). So as an example, 'I'm really excited about our prospects' (nothing to worry about, no obstacles) is less powerful as a piece of disclosure than 'I just don't know how we're going to get through the next few weeks' (lots to worry about, plenty of obstacles).

• But there's great power to be had from combining the two: 'I really don't know **how** (EMPHASIS) we're going to get through the next few weeks PAUSE but I'm **really** excited about the opportunity we have.' Now *that* would make an intriguing start to a story, wouldn't it? But it has to be done with real performance ability, using performance energy. I always remember the senior partner of one of the Big Four accountancy firms I'd been working with taking the stage at the annual partners' conference and opening with the words 'I know you're all feeling apprehensive and insecure – well, I share that with you.' Strange positioning for a leader, you may think; but it won everyone over instantly.

• Don't be afraid to use humour – self-deprecating is usually best, as this is a strong way of bringing people on side with you. Avoid using other people as the butt of your humour though – unless you're a comedian with the special rights that brings.

• Like anything this powerful, self-disclosure isn't without risk. It invites judgement. If the disclosure is skilful and appropriate and serves the common good then it's likely to be judged favourably; but if it's self-important, self-centred or simply intended to shock it will backfire (and probably isn't real disclosure anyway).

The more you work with personal disclosure the more instinctively you'll begin to incorporate it into what you say. To the point that you'll probably come to realise, as I have, that disclosure isn't a tick-box thing, something that's limited to a few opening remarks in a presentation or meeting. In actual fact personal disclosure

is a constant; it is always present because it's embedded in how you look, how you sound and what you say, in a transparent performance of you. Which is why it's such a great source of material, because 'You' is something you know intimately and confidently. It's sharing at a high level: you give, you get back.

Personal disclosure is embedded in how you look, how you sound and what you say, in a transparent performance of you.

Theme and message

To target our story as effectively as we can, to use it most productively to get ourselves and our message across to that person or those people, we need a **theme**. Identifying the right theme means finding out a bit about our audience, obviously, because it needs to be related to them and to resonate with where they are in their thinking and feeling.

Imagine that you're talking to a group of people who are facing an important challenge. You believe they're perfectly capable of meeting it: they're a determined and courageous bunch. But in the past they've shown themselves to be perhaps rather too stubborn and dogged, to the extent that they keep banging away in the same direction even when it's getting them nowhere, and they'd stand a far better chance of success by taking stock and redirecting their efforts. What would be a **theme** appropriate for that particular audience? How about using Socrates' definition of courage – 'intelligent perseverance' – which extols the virtue of perseverance, but also of knowing when it makes sense to change tack? Now that should resonate with them. And it gives us a lovely clear pathway to go down, which means we can start to feel safer because we know where we're going, what we're doing and how it's going to impact on our audience. We've got a theme that starts to give our story real shape. Other possible themes could include dedication, tradition, challenge, trust, collaboration...

Closely allied to theme is the idea of **message**. Think carefully about what message you want to leave people with. It's very frustrating to spend time listening to someone and come away at the end without knowing what the point of it was. But do bear in mind that a message isn't a one-way street. It's not just about what you want to say; it's also about how your audience (whether in a meeting, presentation or conversation) is likely to feel about it, how they're going to receive it. What they're going to *think* based on how they're *feeling* and what they're likely to go away and *do* as a result. As should now be apparent, how they feel and think isn't dictated just by what you say, but is influenced by every aspect of how you look, how you sound, how well you control the arena you're in and how effectively you manage the balance between the intellectual and the emotional aspects of your message and the situation.

That completes the centre and the first spoke of the Storywheel:

FEELING

THEME

MESSAGE

EMOTIONAL
ENERGY
EXPRESSED

YOU

EMOTIONAL
OWNERSHIP

Personal disclosure
using I statement

The next spoke is:

Plot – the 'why' and 'how'

In the theatre plot is everything. It's what drives the narrative, so that we get involved and follow the journey of the character/s and the challenges, pitfalls, conflicts, crises, successes and disasters they experience. A plot typically comprises a series of mini crises and resolutions that grow in a crescendo as the story unfolds, and culminate in a massive conflict and final resolution and the return to a new stability and order. This is what's known as the 'narrative arc'. It holds the audience on an emotional rollercoaster that swings between elation and despair (and a whole spectrum of emotions in between), and it's what hooks us in and keeps us on the journey, even if we already know the end. But if the plot is too complex and confusing the audience will eventually disengage, however well performed the play is. Performing in Shakespeare plays was always my favourite, as his ability to present us with a very clear and powerful plotline while at the same time weaving in complex human behaviour, always using beautiful and evocative language, produces the best framework for an actor and director – it's all in there; all you have to do is decide how you want to interpret it for yourself.

When I was rehearsing the part of Lady Macbeth, I realised the extent to which her character was the key to her ultimate tragedy: she was on a path of self-destruction. Shakespeare takes you relentlessly down that path and it starts to drive the narrative. You know at a deep level that she is not going to end up well – but at the same time you think that she just might. But this is the power of the plot: its path must be clear, but full of 'moments', some good, some not, that hold our focus and attention right to the end. The very best dramas will enthral us even though we know the ending. We may know how Shakespeare's plays end, but does it stop us wanting to see different productions? No. This is the power of the story, and the framework that holds it all together is the plot.

'The battle was won' – a statement.
'Why and how I won the battle' – a plot.

You can take any situation, scenario or drama that is currently unfolding in your life and apply the 'why and how' principle to it. This will quickly give you a plot and consequently a framework for a story. Without the why and the how we have no story, because there's no purpose or journey – and these are fundamental to any narrative, whether spoken or written.

I'm not suggesting you need to put together a James Bond or Bridget Jones style plot every time you speak. Just that you stay aware of what it takes to hold an audience's interest in terms of how you structure what you say and the content you use. Here's a simple way of turning your situation (interview, presentation, pitch, conversation or whatever) into a plot with the beginnings of a narrative arc: answer the following questions:

• Who am I?
• What do I want?
• What challenges stand in my way?
• How will/did I resolve them?

This simple framework has helped many a CEO or senior executive I've worked with focus and carve out an address to their company or team, keeping themselves authentically at the centre. It's very powerful and personal and really lands with people. I'm not saying that you have to use this format for everything you do, but it will give you a solid platform until you find your feet and can start experimenting with different approaches (but remember, whatever your approach, you are at the centre of it and must not hide). Try thinking about a situation or a story you want to tell by answering the questions above, and using your answers as your structure (or your 'narrative arc'). Here's a bit more flesh on the bones to help you:

• Who am I? What are my characteristics or personality traits that are particularly relevant to this story (you may find it easier to decide on these once you've answered the other questions!)?
• What did I want to achieve, what was my heart's desire?
• What stood in my way?
• How did I confront and overcome these obstacles and challenges?

Expand on this with some follow-up questions:
• What have been some of the failures along the way, and what have I learned from these? Failure is an essential part of success – and remember that a tale without setback and failure is unbelievable and boring.
• What did my ultimate success/achievement look and feel like?

• What have I learned about myself/other people by going through this process, how have I grown, what is the new position I've reached and what is the view of the world from here?

This approach takes as its basis the idea that, when you boil it right down, plot is about character. The plot of just about any story you can think of is fundamentally about someone who wants something, is prevented from getting it, and how their character responds to a series of challenges and obstacles until they ultimately prevail and get the object of their desire: the person they love, the ring with the magical powers, justice for a cause, the overthrow of an evil empire, slaying the dragon...

'Hmm,' I hear you thinking. 'Plot is character. That's all very well in a story, but how does it apply in real life?' Well, real life is no different. For example, what people want to hear when they're listening to an investment professional who's looking after millions of pounds of their money is, at its heart, very personal. They want to know what makes this person tick, can they be trusted, what will drive their investment decisions (for example, do they sound as though they have an abnormal need to prove something, which might make them reckless?); if there's a downturn, will they be cool and tough enough to follow their strategy; are they someone who will involve us in their thinking, or will they just expect us to show them complete faith and let them get on with it, no questions asked?

In the same vein, what we want to hear in an apology from someone who's treated us badly is not, on the whole, a bald 'Sorry'; what makes an apology count for something is when we are given some understanding of what prompted the person to behave in the way they did, what they were having to deal with at the time, their perspective on the situation, what they'd found out about themselves in the process, what they'd resolved to change – wishful thinking perhaps, but that on the whole has far more credibility and meaning than just a grunted 'Sorry'.

A couple of big advantages of the 'plot is character' idea are:

1. It's easy to remember! And...
2. It will launch you, almost automatically, into a strong piece of personal disclosure. I guarantee you'll come up with something about yourself and the situation that will be arresting, and that will give you an injection of performance energy that will power you into your performance.

Now I'm not saying that you have to talk about *yourself* the whole time. There is no limit to who you can include in the cast: family, friends, people you meet along the way, or – in a business context – the people you work with, your team, your organisation as a whole. But a strong 'I' statement is a great starting point, and 'I' is an essential character to make the story live. I often get pushback on this from my business clients, who feel that bringing themselves into business presentations or meetings is not the 'done thing'; and while the mood is gradually shifting in some quarters, there is still a reluctance to bring individuality and personality into business. This self-effacement is drummed into people through sayings such as 'There's no "I" in "team"'; well, there's no 'We' either, come to that. So stop hiding and come out and show yourself – figuratively and sometimes literally, it's *you* we've paid to see!

The Theatre Wheel: 'The Show's the Thing!'
The professional theatre offers a great model for teamwork.
It works with a reality that applies equally in the world of
business: not everyone likes each other or naturally gets on.
The key to building a great team is *not* to try to smooth out the
differences, but rather to bring strong, talented and *different*
people together in a tight ensemble. There should be *lots* of
'I' in team! Without wishing to run you over with wheels, it's a
model I call the 'Theatre Wheel'...

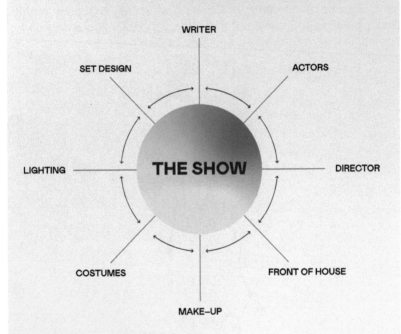

Any theatre production involves lots of different people all
doing different things (there are loads more than I could fit
into the diagram). Often they don't get on. Many of them think
they're more important than anyone else. But they all have to
work accurately and with a high level of detail, and they know
that they have to communicate along parallel lines in order
for the show to happen – and that they'll be hugely exposed
if their part isn't aligned to the overall destination when the
curtain goes up. The show drives everything. It demands and
develops collaboration and great teamwork.

You may find it helpful to have a tighter framework into which to fit this unfolding of character. In his brilliant book The Seven Basic Plots, Christopher Booker identifies the following pool of plots that encompass all stories:

1. Overcoming the Monster – for example, *Harry Potter*
2. Rags to Riches – *Great Expectations*
3. The Quest – *The Hobbit*
4. Voyage and Return – *The Wizard of Oz*
5. Comedy – *Four Weddings and a Funeral*
6. Tragedy – *Macbeth*
7. Rebirth – *A Christmas Carol*

These plotlines can be very useful as a benchmark and possible vehicle for your own story, and can provide a good canvas for the story of your character(s) to play out on. They can be a great way to define where you are and the challenges you face, and give you conscious clarification. Whenever I ask a business client which of the plots resonates most with them and best describes where they or their company are, they always know immediately.

For example, in a business context *Overcoming the Monster* might provide a very useful vehicle for the story of a company's fightback against the odds, or of a strategy to beat a competitor; *Rebirth* could be a good fit for a business embracing the digital age, or for implementing an HR initiative to re-engage employees. I recently helped a client in a specialist niche within the banking sector put together a roadshow to take round to all its offices, to communicate their strategy to their employees. I'd been struck by an account I'd heard by journalist and author Malcolm Gladwell of the David and Goliath story, which gave me a much deeper insight into the story's real complexity and made it far more intriguing.

In Gladwell's analysis, far from being a huge long shot that David would defeat the giant, it was in fact an inevitable outcome. David was a skilled marksman and could, from a safe distance, take deadly aim with his slingshot, against which the lumbering Goliath was defenceless. The heavily armoured and massively strong Goliath was only effective in close-up hand-to-hand slugging matches with opponents who adopted a similar approach. This story was a great framework for my client's message, and helped instil in her audiences the confidence that they could defeat much larger competitors with their precisely targeted, agile and skilfully executed strategy. So play around, make links, draw on anything around you for inspiration and make notes of anything you come across that you think you might be able to use in some way. The only limit to your use of story is your imagination.

 I'm proud of the work I've done for dyslexia, not just raising money, but helping young people in prison as well as some of our most brilliant entrepreneurs and business leaders. My methodology has been very successful in challenging and loosening the straitjacket that people often feel trapped in when they can't follow linear communication, either written or spoken. Dyslexia has little to do with levels of intelligence, either IQ or EQ, but a great deal to do with thinking and communicating differently. People with dyslexia have a tendency to focus too much on the precise detail of their content, because they're constantly frightened of getting it 'wrong' and not being understood. This usually means they get stuck trying to work with a linear process that is essentially alien to them, and in so doing lose their magical creativity and spontaneity. This is where my mantra 'freedom within a framework' is especially helpful to many of them.

I took part in a special programme for young prison inmates with dyslexia, working in three prisons in the south of England. I would get the boys up to 'tell a story', film them and work on some simple techniques with them. It transformed how they saw each other and how they felt about themselves, and brought home to me yet again that story provides the framework and the structure that supports the freedom to express ourselves.

I have gradually realised that this process can help anyone to feel safe and stay on message, while still having the freedom to extemporise and bring their personality to the fore and use whatever words they need in the moment, without having the panic of trying to read a script, remember their lines or look at their notes. Using this method I have helped hundreds of men and women, young and old alike, dyslexic or not, find their truth and fluency.

So now the Storywheel looks like this:

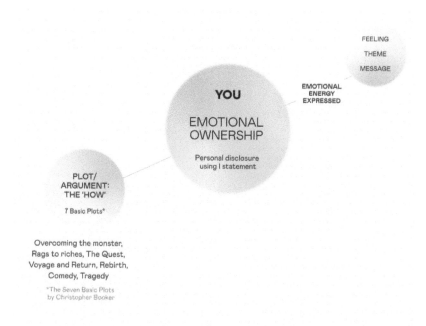

Structure

As we've already seen, plot works hand in glove with the drama's structure or 'narrative arc'. In essence, the structure of the narrative arc denotes the story's beginning, middle and end.

The **Beginning** introduces the main character and the situation, and sets up the conflict between what the protagonist wants and what stands in their way; this is the 'hook' that ignites our interest and makes us want to know more. The **Middle** is the narrative purpose, it's what gives the story shape and direction. And then what do I want to leave them with?

What is the **End**? Is it an arrival, i.e. OK, please yourself, go away and think about what this means to you; or is it a conclusion: this is what this is about, take it away and act on it?

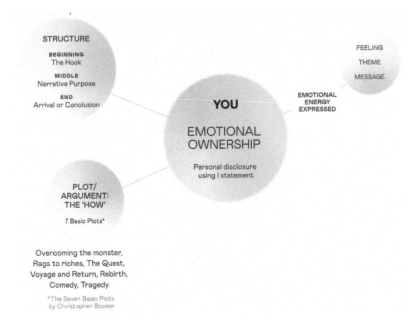

STRUCTURE

BEGINNING
The Hook

MIDDLE
Narrative Purpose

END
Arrival or Conclusion

PLOT/ ARGUMENT: THE 'HOW'

7 Basic Plots*

Overcoming the monster,
Rags to riches, The Quest,
Voyage and Return, Rebirth,
Comedy, Tragedy

*The Seven Basic Plots
by Christopher Booker

YOU

EMOTIONAL OWNERSHIP

Personal disclosure
using I statement

FEELING

THEME

MESSAGE

EMOTIONAL ENERGY EXPRESSED

Images, anecdotes, examples

Now we've got to a point where emotional energy is beginning to make the Storywheel turn; we have a theme and an idea of how the plot and structure are going to work… but that's not enough, is it? Something's missing. Think about how incredibly powerful radio is – and why? Because it needs you to create all your own images in your imagination.

OK, how do we paint pictures in people's heads in a very simple story form?

Your story will inevitably contain people, places and things – so describe them; give your listener some understanding of who and what they are, of what it feels like to be in a particular place. Use anecdotes and examples to bring them to life. Describe as well as explain. Paint pictures in people's minds. Make them sticky: a sensory perception – a visual, taste or smell – associated with a feeling is what we remember the most (as famously exemplified by Proust's madeleine experience). If you're in a place that demands lots of information and where people expect jargon, fine: just underpin it with a 'For instance', an anecdote, mini-stories, an example that comes from you. In the words of Anton Chekhov, 'Don't tell me the moon is shining; show me the glint of light on broken glass.'

'Don't tell me the moon is shining; show me the glint of light on broken glass.'

Anton Chekhov

And that completes the Storywheel...

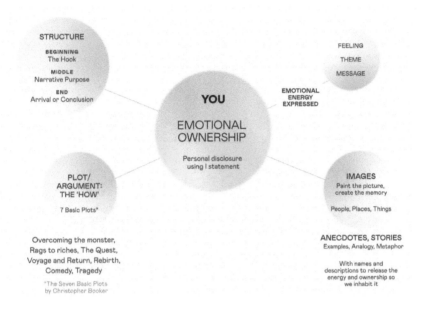

These are the really important things about story. It isn't just for presentations, it's for one-to-one, it's for anywhere. It's for your life. Working with the Storywheel will change your approach to communicating with people in a profound way. It's very common for people to plan their communication (if they plan it at all) in terms of a tick-list, making sure that they've got down all the points they want to cover without actually thinking about the other person and what will make things work for *them*, what will resonate with them, how they will best remember things. The Storywheel is an important ingredient in making your communication work for other people. It does a very specific job: it's a tool for getting your generic material in place, leaving you free to finesse it for the nuances and needs of different audiences. Later in the book we'll be examining how you do this, looking more closely at TFD (what you want whomever you're talking with to **Think**, **Feel** and **Do**) and working with Aimapping (a framework for strategising your message, your audience, the situation and you in it).

SUMMARY CHAPTER 6

• Human beings can't resist a story – it's a very powerful communication tool.

• Story is a great framework to channel performance energy and to plan your life.

• The key components of the Storywheel are:

• Personal disclosure: energises the wheel and connects you with yourself and the audience.

• Plot: drives the narrative arc and keeps the audience hooked. It's largely driven by character. A simple model:
- Who am I?
- What do I want?
- What challenges lie in my way?
- How will/did I resolve them?

• Theme: helps target the story to a specific audience. Some triggers for you: courage, perseverance, dedication, tradition, challenge, trust, collaboration...

• Structure: Beginning, Middle and End.

• Images, examples, anecdotes: *describe*. This brings your story to life and makes it real and memorable.

Things to work on
Use your You brand diary to note down anything you come across that you think you might be able to use as part of a story: an analogy, metaphor, something that's happened to you that illustrates a point. Look for patterns, practise making links. Exercise your story-making and storytelling muscles as much as you can. Observe how much story is used in conversation; and how it's used. Practise out loud in front of the mirror.

CHAPTER 7

Telling the Story: How to Prepare

'You are always one decision away from a totally different life.'
Anon.

This chapter may not give you a totally different life, but it will hopefully give you a totally different approach to preparing for a presentation, meeting or interview.

This is a three-stage process:

2nd Stage	1st Stage	3rd Stage
Work out your 'pontoons': right-brain 'triggers'	Use your Storywheel: it will give you the spine, the narrative purpose, the story: do this first!	Add in visuals or images to help tell the story – but only if they really add value!

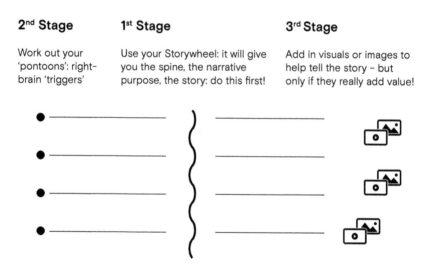

1st stage
Create the narrative, i.e. the story, which we've just been exploring in the last chapter. This is the backbone, the spine; without it you have nowhere to go. Start with personal disclosure to get the energy going for you, to connect to your content with ownership and belief and to invite your audience in – this is your petrol: emotional energy expressed.

2nd stage
Once the story has real flow, meaning and direction (your message) – it'll take shape after a few practice runs – the next stage is to extract from the narrative simple **triggers** or 'pontoons' that will help you remember where you are going and keep you on track while you are telling your story: a visual image, an important fact, an emotional emphasis, a change of thought or subject.

3rd stage
The final part of the process of putting your story together is deciding whether you need any visuals to help you tell the story or to add value to it. You may need nothing at all; the most effective visuals are the ones you paint inside people's heads through the characters, places and things that you describe and the stories you tell.

Sound unlikely? Bear this in mind: in theatre, the actors in a play only get their lighting, costumes, make-up and props towards the very end of the rehearsal process. The philosophy is that the play would, fundamentally, work without these, just through the power of storytelling and the actors' performances.

Many people use memorising, scripts, notes or bullet points to help them with presentations and other forms of public speaking. So why am I not recommending any of these? Quite simply, because they hinder communication rather than help it. Here's why ...

Memorising
Apart from being time-consuming, memorising what you're going to say can put you in a precarious position. If you forget your lines, or get lost in them, it can be very hard if not impossible to get back on track. And unless you know how to perform, the audience will quickly spot that you're working from memory, and this will detract from the all-important feeling that what you are saying is spontaneous, heartfelt and real, and just for them.

Stilted scripts
The way we write and the way we speak are very different. That's why a script – unless written by a professional scriptwriter and performed by a professional actor – so often comes over as wooden and stilted, rather than spontaneous and genuine.
If someone's reading, they can't mean it (at least that's the subliminal message, which is reinforced by the fact that they're likely to perform it badly to boot); if someone else has written it, then they *really* can't mean it; and if it's written it's unlikely to work out of someone's mouth in any case.

No use notes

People using notes tend to make them too long and too linear. This means that, to make sense of them, you have to read them pretty much in full, when all you've got time for in the heat of the moment is a quick glance. So if you lose your way, notes like these are worse than useless, and are likely set you off into a flother of paper shuffling and awkwardness. Reading is a cognitive left-brain process that takes time, whereas to work well a prompt needs to allow instant right-brain access.

Pointless bullet points

Bullet points are roughly the same as notes – the only difference being that they're projected onto a big screen for everyone to see. They encourage the speaker to turn their back on the audience and read from them. They split focus: the audience doesn't know whether to read or to listen, and usually ends up doing neither. When putting them together, in order to make them appear concise and important, people tend to concentrate as much meaning as possible into each word. And then the speaker's brain (not to mention the brains of the poor people they're talking to, who have to read the stuff) has to *work it all out* – which just takes too long. The result is that bullet points are pretty much meaningless. They're not helpful for the audience: they have no clear narrative and they completely distract people from what the speaker is saying. And they're certainly no good for the speaker as a guide to where they're going next, as they block any kind of flow.

Instead of all of this, I urge you to use pontoons.

Pontoons

What are pontoons and why should I use them instead?

'Pontoons' is my You brand name for short phrases or even single words that will trigger you into the next part of your story. Pontoons sit happily in the right – intuitive – hemisphere of the brain, from where information can be accessed at a glance in the heat of the moment. They come from the narrative spine of your story.

I call them pontoons because they can be thought of as floating platforms that you can 'tie up to' at various points without restricting or constraining your journey. Instead you can navigate confidently through your story knowing that you have safe but flexible reminders of where you are now and where you're going. This, incidentally, is how prompting works in the theatre. Actors are prompted by just one or two words, which enables them to

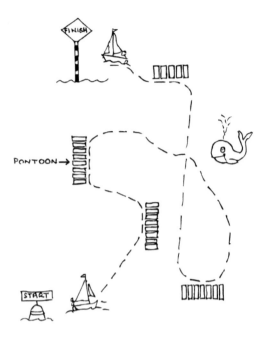

remember their line – get the next part of the jigsaw – very fast. Being fed a whole line, by contrast, would take actors into the processing part of their brain and likely make them freeze.

I like to lay out my pontoons like this – words or short phrases with an arrow linking to the next one:

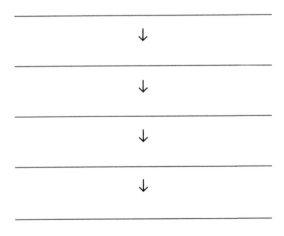

To give you the idea, the process I went through in preparing my Dyslexia Awards speech involved a couple of stages of pontooning. At first they looked like this:

Tent In Kenya

↓

Vice-Captain of Green Team!

↓

Badge in Bed

↓

Feeling Recognised:
Nothing Came Close Before or Since

↓

Misfit

↓

7 Moves by 7

↓

Cold Village Schools

↓

Bullied

↓

Alone in Playground

↓

Badge = Worth Something

After I'd practised a bit, the only pontoons I needed to stay on track were these:

Tent In Kenya

↓

Vice-Captain of Green Team!

↓

Badge in Bed – Wow !!!

↓

Recognized

↓

Misfit

↓

<u>7</u> Moves by 7

↓

Badge = *Worth* Something. Happy!

I use different colours, underlining and exclamation marks etc. as emotional nudges and pointers; it helps create flow (it's what we do in the theatre when we're marking up a script in rehearsal). Play around to find whatever works best for you.

Slides, visual aids and other support material – and how to make them work for you.
Slides and other forms of 'visual aids' are widely used in speeches and presentations, especially in an office or work context. But just how effective are they?

When preparing to present in front of an audience we often start with slides, because we feel that 'content' is the easiest aspect of a presentation to work on; and sorting out a bunch of slides makes us feel that we've done some solid preparation. Or else someone's given us a 'company standard' presentation deck to use and follow.

It's all too easy to fall into such traps without really thinking through the impact we wish to have on our audience, and what it's *really* going to take to achieve that. Slides and visual aids will only support your story if they're part of an integrated and emotionally intelligent structure. They are never a substitute for *You*.

Having said that, slides and visuals (decks, brochures etc.) can be useful; you just need to understand how to make them work for you. There are three ways to achieve this.

Divisible

Make an informal introduction to what you're going to be talking about, give your audience the big picture overview, influencing them in terms of how you want them to understand and feel about the information or idea you're presenting, and 'selling you'. *Then* give them a brief factual reinforcement of what you've said, keeping it as simple and visual as possible, using a quick run-through of slides, a deck, a handout, brochure or some other leave-behind. This will reinforce their perception that your opinions and ideas are based in solid research and fact.

Integrated

Here the slides are an integral part of your presentation. You speak for a while, then put up a slide to illustrate or expand on a point you've just made; speak some more, put up another slide, and so on.

To bring real energy and a feeling of spontaneity and interaction into the slide process, try actually drawing them up by hand on a flipchart as you go. They may not be as manicured as pre-prepared slides, but the audience will find the process a lot more engaging.

Don't allow the slide to pull focus – that is, to deflect attention from you. When you put a slide up, make it the centre of attention: focus the audience on it, tell them which particular part of the slide to look at (point to it or touch it if possible) and say what it means. Give people enough time to take in the information on the slide, then *turn it off* and take the focus back to you. Don't leave it on in the background: put up the company logo or another neutral image – or nothing – instead. Our eyes are naturally drawn to light, so if you leave up a slide that people can read you'll lose your audience. If you present the audience with a split focus they will be drawn to the light of the slide and simply take in information from it, without the filter of anything you may be saying – which can influence how they read it. They may take away an interpretation that's very different from the one you want.

Theatrical

Theatrical or 'sleight of hand' use of slides is a great option when your subject is highly technical. Tell the audience that you have a huge number of slides or a large amount of supporting information – or, for even greater impact, give them a glimpse of them all together on the screen in preview mode – to demonstrate you've done your homework and know your content in the minutest detail. Then tell them you won't be using the slides as there's too much to get through (and listen to the collective sigh of relief!) and say what you have to say, pulling out the main points and your view and interpretation of the data – which is what you're there to do, after all. You can always offer your audience access to a copy of the slides afterwards if they want to study them at their leisure.

All of this is about putting you in control of your visual aids (rather than the other way round) while subliminally managing audience expectations. Which method you use will depend on the specifics of the situation and the choices you make about your material and the audience.

SUMMARY CHAPTER 7

• Follow the three-stage process when you're constructing
a story to deliver:
- Work out the narrative.
- Use your pontoons to keep you on track while allowing you
the freedom to roam around.
- Decide on which, if any, visual aids or props to use.
With this you'll be able to create a pathway entirely fitted
to the audience or occasion, around which you can easily
extemporise. You'll have freedom within a framework, which
is hugely powerful.

• Resist any temptation to change this order of preparation.

• Scripts, notes and bullet points will weaken your story and
your delivery of it; use the Storywheel and pontoons instead.

• Only use slides and visual aids if they add value and help
tell your story – not as a prompt or crutch. And think about
the way in which you will use them: integrated, divisible or
theatrical.

Things to work on
If you normally use slides, the next time you have a
presentation to give, try doing it without any slides at all –
see where it takes you. But make sure to do your Storywheel,
and practise it walking around and *out loud*! You may find it
helpful to practise in front of a mirror. Make sure to get your
pontoons clear and that they work at a glance – and use
pause and emphasis to buy yourself the time to use them
fluently, and for your message and meaning to land.

CHAPTER 8

Using All the Tools So Far

'Practice does not make perfect.
Only perfect practice makes perfect.'
Vince Lombardi

Now I want you to bring together everything we've done so far. We have an understanding of performance energy (our fuel), story structure and pontoons (to navigate with), pause, emphasis and the Variety Pack (for pace, meaning, light, shade and tone). Soon I'm going to ask you to put all of this together to structure and perform a piece.

But before you do that, I'd like to introduce you to some important vocal and physical warm-up exercises that will help bring your mind, heart and body together, and provide you with a strong platform from which to perform. These exercises will help you to:

• achieve a conscious alignment of your tools of communication: your head, heart and body.
• prepare for a scary situation.
• bring disabling nerves under control.
• reframe anxiety as excitement.
• get into a mindful state so you can be 'in the moment'.

… all very useful, I'm sure you'd agree. The exercises are quick and easy to practise – and practice is essential. So, step 1…

Find a space suitable for doing energetic physical warm-ups.

• Breathe deeply from the diaphragm for about twenty seconds. A good test to check you are breathing from the right place (your diaphragm) is to put your hand on your tummy. Stick it *out* (fat tummy) as you breathe in, then draw it in as you breathe out. Sounds a bit counterintuitive, I know, but practise slowly and consciously and you will get it, I promise. In bed is a good place to practise, as it's easy to relax lying down. Think of your tummy as a pair of bellows, sucking air in as you pull the handles apart and blowing it out as you squeeze them together. And remember to keep breathing from your diaphragm throughout these exercises!

• With your arm bent and fingertips on your shoulder, circle each arm forwards and backwards, one at a time.

• Roll your head gently from side to side.

• Lift both shoulders right up to your ears and then let them fall. You may be surprised at how far they fall! We hold a great deal of tension in our neck and shoulders, and releasing it is essential as otherwise it will constrict the vocal cords and make your voice sound thin and unengaging.

• Plant your feet firmly hip distance apart and shake yourself out.

• Drop gently to the floor from your waist, with soft knees. Let your head fall forward, shake your arms out and do a little bounce. Relax every muscle!

• Very gradually start to come back up as you breathe into your diaphragm – not your chest! Feel every breath raising you a little more. Keep the breath deep and connected to you physically. Let your head hang loose. It's important that you do all of this very slowly, as you can hyperventilate if you come up too quickly.

• Once you're back in a standing position, imagine that there is a silver thread attached to the top of your head gently pulling your head to a very balanced position at the top of your spine.

• Test your shoulders again: up to your ears, and down.

This next exercise is one you can do anywhere, any time.

• Take off your shoes (and your socks if the situation allows). With your feet hip distance apart and hands relaxed by your sides, drop your head and look at your toes.

• Spread your toes so they really connect to the floor.

• Now rock gently onto the balls of your feet, keeping your heels on the floor.

• Close your eyes and feel the floor with your feet. Focus on that for thirty seconds. Now imagine your feet are connected to the level below – the floorboards under the carpet or the concrete – and feel that for thirty seconds.

• Now feel that connection down through to the earth, focusing all the time on your breath moving in and out from the diaphragm and your relaxed shoulders, and start to sense how 'rooted' you feel – nothing can push you off course or undermine your strength and confidence. Your whole being is now connected physically and emotionally, your mind empty of anxiety and stress. Do this for another sixty seconds, then gradually let your head come up, pulled gently up by the silver cord, and breathe out.

• Now take a gentle breath in through your diaphragm, open your mouth – and speak.

This is brilliant for settling nerves just before you start a presentation or speech, or before going into an important meeting, interview or difficult conversation. Many of my top speakers and CEOs around the world have learned this technique and still use it. Two or three minutes max, and you'll be ready for the fray.

Now for one minute of **mindful meditation**. This you can do as a quick fix just before you go into any stressful situation:

• Close your eyes and breathe in from the diaphragm, hold for a count of six and then breathe out slowly. Follow your breath. Do this for six breaths in and six out. Focus everything on your breath to keep your mind from straying to anxiety or filling with voices.

• Relax your shoulders and check them – up to your ears and down; shake them out.

• Take a breath, and in you go! You are ready and in the moment, where you need to be – not in your head!

(You might like to try the app *Calm*, which, at the time of writing, was voted the best meditation app by a Facebook poll.)

When I was at drama school this process would be drilled into us every day to get our whole being ready for the challenging task of being on stage. Before every show you will find actors on stage warming up their tools (!), doing voice exercises and mental relaxation in preparation for doing their job; so why should it be any different for you? Why wouldn't you keep your body, mind and emotional connectedness in a place of peak condition in order to do the professional job of performing You?

So now I want you to put together everything you've learned so far and use it to structure and perform a piece. This might be an upcoming presentation you have to give; or maybe you have a job interview coming up. Or perhaps you know you've got a serious and important conversation to have with someone.

 Think back to the first piece you did to camera in Chapter 4. Then, with your upcoming 'performance' in mind, sit down quietly and fill in your Storywheel so that you have a beginning, middle and end; and the all-important 'I' statement with personal disclosure to release energy and create a pathway that you can own and follow.

To give you an example, this is what I used in my Dyslexia Awards speech:

'I' statement disclosure: 'I have always felt like an outsider, different.'
Feeling: sad, lonely, turning into happiness.
Theme: exclusion, recognition, acceptance.
Message: Who you are is valuable; have faith; it's OK to be you.

Images: the badge, the tent, the bedroom, darkness, mobile, the little girl.
Plot: how I got my badge and found my self-esteem.
Structure:
Beginning (the hook): I have always felt like an outsider, different. I was in a tent in Kenya...
Middle: me as a schoolgirl.
End: I found acceptance (distinguish between 'arrival' – here we all are, what do you think? – seed planting – and 'conclusion': this is where we are, act on it).

Another example: the personal disclosure 'I' statement could be 'I was terrified'; the theme: courage; the message or moral: never quit; and the plot: 'how I/we won the deal/pitch/battle/game/negotiation'. Use images and anecdotes, a 'for instance' that will create a visual memory and support your meaning. Think about how you might take your audience on a rollercoaster ride of nervous anticipation, an early success followed by a setback, how everything seemed hopeless until you steeled yourself to the task and pulled out all the stops until you finally won through.

A tendency I find with many of my clients is that when they do their first piece to camera they talk about their job in list form – they recite all their roles and responsibilities without giving any sense of the excitement, fulfilment, frustrations or challenges they experience. This is entirely self-imposed – they haven't been asked to take this approach – and can be explained, I think, as people playing safe when the feeling of exposure kicks in. So please don't fall into this trap. Let your hair down and your imagination run wild...

Now walk around the room speaking out loud your ideas and thoughts within your story framework. It's very important to get the words out of your mouth, so don't miss this out. **Remember: we don't speak the way we think, we don't speak the way we write – we speak the way we speak.** Remember to use twice the energy you feel comfortable with – and half the pace!

Practise until it feels right and your story pathway is working. A new neural pathway will be forming – this is your framework!

From this, extract four or five key pontoons and write them on a card or piece of paper, like this:

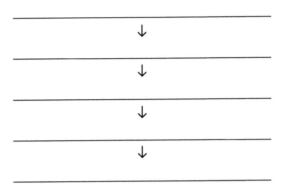

Refer back to the example in the last chapter if you get stuck.

'When the greatest of all the Greek orators, Demosthenes, was asked what the three most important skills were for a speaker, he replied "Delivery, delivery and delivery."
Michael Trapp, Professor of Greek Literature and Thought, King's College London

Write the pontoons on the dotted lines; the spaces in between (the arrows) will align with the right brain and will not disrupt the flow by pushing your brain into processing mode. They will act as an at-a-glance prompt that can be absorbed immediately and, with practice, they will remove you from the need to learn lines, or use complicated notes or visual aids, and leave you free to deliver. Demosthenes would have been delighted.

Using pontoons is where the pause really comes into its own. Hit on a 'travelling' or 'bridging' word or phrase such as 'so', 'now', 'of course' or 'however', using a good bucket of energy on the word, then pause... look at your pontoon list (placed on a convenient table, stool or plant stand nearby)... and find your link... and another bucket of energy on the next word you come in on... and carry on. No one will mind, or probably even notice, that you've taken a look at your pontoons, as using pause and emphasis to buy yourself time looks quite natural and normal, gives pace and integrity to your performance and shows a considered approach to your subject. In no way does it make the audience feel uncomfortable or worried for you.

It's a win-win. But you must stay in the performance energy zone to make it work.

Now set up your camera. Give yourself space and find the width of the camera frame you have to move around in – remember, you don't have to stay rooted to the spot. Breathe from the diaphragm, using **twice the energy** you feel comfortable with from a standing start, and **half the pace** – and tell your story. Use harmonious movement whenever you change pace or thought. Use your hands to support and express, and **emphasis** to buy the pause.

It's helpful to think about movement and use of space like this: imagine you're standing in a semicircle – your 'playing area' – with the audience along the flat side or 'baseline'. If you think of your position like this, you can only move backwards from the baseline. This is negative, 'filling the gap' movement that is reactive. It conveys to the audience the equivalent of an 'um' or 'er'.

AUDIENCE

Instead, turn the semicircle round...

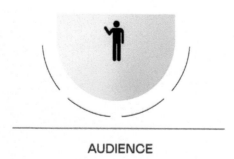

AUDIENCE

Use twice the
energy you feel
comfortable
with from a
standing start,
and half
the pace.

... and see how you can move *forward* from the baseline, or side to side, and come to a stop in the middle. The space becomes proactive and conveys to the audience confidence and connectedness.

Build to your end and leave us with a message. This is like music: you need to signal with pace and build that you are coming to an end and that the final takeaway is worth waiting for. Sustain the energy right through to the end – and then make it *land*. Your audience will feel that they have 'met **you**'.

WELL DONE!

Now play this performance back and start to critique yourself – but from an aware, professional perspective, because now you know what to look for.

Now do it again! Keep that energy up, using pause and emphasis all the time. Try different words and descriptive phrases; you don't have to use or memorise the same words; you can just keep the golden thread of theme and plot clear and sustained.

And AGAIN!

Can you feel the freedom? Isn't it wonderful? And *You* are now visible.

Now try it for real!
It's one thing to be reading about all of this in a book, and trying things out on your own in front of a camera. But a really important part of the learning process is to use all of this out there in the big wide normal world. Just take small baby steps to start with, in whatever situations you find yourself in – close-up one-to-ones, whether physically present or virtual, or bigger spaces with a few more people if you get the chance – and see and reflect on how you feel. You may think, 'I used my hands consciously and expressively with more energy and felt fine and no one laughed!' or, 'I consciously used the pause to help my words to land, so the meaning became clearer; and I found that the pause gave me more time to decide "how" to say things.'

You may well receive feedback, which means that you are being noticed and having an impact, that you *look* more confident and congruent and are more visible. Hopefully you will find that your posture is more energised so you are physically more present. I strongly urge you to make a note of these things in your **You brand** notebook, along with your observations of others, what you notice in their behaviour and how you react to them – little things, perhaps, but significant.

Some tips to bear in mind and try out...

• Remember to shake hands firmly and confidently with people – but don't crush their fingers.

• Make and hold eye contact appropriately: it communicates openness, trustworthiness and sincerity and can add hugely to the power of what you say. Don't stare though.

• If you're sitting, sit upright on your sitting bones. Don't slouch. What feels comfortable can look arrogant, dismissive or sloppy – and is a bad posture for performing well.

• If you're at a desk or table, sit with a distance of 18–24" between your tummy and the table. This avoids you becoming locked behind or on the table, and gives you performance space to use your arms and hands to gesture freely.

• Lean forward occasionally to indicate that you're really listening to what the other person is saying.

Actively seek out opportunities to put together and deliver a presentation or webinar; go for that interview; stop putting off that difficult conversation; speak up early in the meeting or the weekly Zoom – these are all opportunities to try out and practise what you've been learning. Or simply chat to people, but using the skills you've been working on. Make a note of how these things go, and how you feel. You may be surprised at the extent to which just approaching these situations in this frame of mind – seeing them as an opportunity to practise – takes the sting out of them and automatically makes them easier and more satisfying.

Do this for about two weeks, then your 'soak' time for this stage of the work is completed and we are ready to go on to the next stage of our quest.

SUMMARY CHAPTER 8

• Put a practice piece together using the Storywheel.
Think about:
- Personal disclosure using an 'I' statement to energise
and create a personal pathway
- Feeling
- Theme
- Message
- Images
- Plot
- Structure: Beginning, Middle, End

• Walk round the room and speak out loud: get the words
out of your mouth.

• When your story pathway feels right, pontoon it.

• Perform it to camera: twice the energy that feels
comfortable, half the pace. Breathe from the diaphragm.
Use your arms and hands to modulate, reinforce and express,
and emphasis to buy the pause.

• Avoid 'negative' (backwards) movement: come forwards
to your imaginary audience.

• Repeat! Keep working at it.

Things to work on
Try all of this out in the real world. Baby steps as you build
your confidence. Actively observe and note down people's
responses, your observations of people, how you feel. Please
don't rush into the next chapter. Take a week or two to try out
all the tools you've been working with so far, remain actively
aware of what you experience. Reflect and digest.

CHAPTER 9

The Desire to Communicate: You *Have* to *Want* to!

'Enthusiasm is one of the most powerful engines of success. When you do a thing do it with all your might. Be active, be energetic, be enthusiastic and faithful, and you will accomplish your objective.'
Ralph Waldo Emerson

'Imagination is the only weapon in the war against reality.'
Jules de Gaultier

Welcome back! Here we are again, after a break to try out what you've learned out there in the real world, both physical and virtual. I hope it's been going well, and that you've begun to feel more confident and less anxious about certain situations than you were when you first picked up this book.

It's very likely that, as you've been experimenting over the last couple of weeks or so, you've felt less motivated to engage with people at certain times or in certain situations than others. And you've probably observed that, when you weren't feeling motivated, your impact and effectiveness in those situations were diminished. And that's completely normal and natural; it happens to everyone. However, in *professional* communication situations (look back to Chapter 4 to remind yourself how we defined 'professional'), we obviously want to do our best to maintain the highest levels of impact and effectiveness at all times.

What exactly are these 'professional' situations? Well in fact it's entirely up to you to decide. It depends when and where you want your communication and impact to be effective and achieve something positive, to persuade and be influential, to leave a genuine and memorable impression... For most of the clients I work with, there are certain situations where consistently strong communication is a no-brainer, completely essential. Most of these are work-related: making presentations; pitching, negotiating, leading or participating in meetings; chairing; interviewing and being interviewed; appearing in the media; speaking at the annual conference... Then there are the less 'set-piece' occasions, such as networking at business 'social' events, mentoring people, motivating, leading or being part of a team and generally interacting with colleagues, partners and clients on a casual day-to-day basis. Holding professional standards of communication may not seem so essential here, but there may still be negative consequences for our relationships, reputation and everyday effectiveness if we drop our level of communication in these situations to 'amateur'.

And then there are those less obvious 'private' situations, where we may feel that we're so accepted for who we are that we don't have to make an effort: how we interact at home, away from work, with friends, family, our husband, wife, partner or children. I've known clients who have reported that their marriage has been saved as a result of what they've learned in their coaching, that their relationships with family and friends have been transformed, that their kids have been wowed by their new way of reading the bedtime story or listening to and better understanding them when they become alien teenage life forms...

One of the important things I hope you'll take from this book is how you manage your own feelings and consequently the feelings of others with a heightened emotional intelligence and skill about *how* you communicate. This will give you conscious *choice* over how you come over, as well as the ability to move into the professional zone at the flick of a switch – your switch that *you* can flick. Over time, you may find that you stay switched on more often than not, and that 'professional' becomes a way of life.

So what is the foundation for professional communication – or for professional anything, come to that? What is the default mindset that has to be in play to keep you in the 70%+ zone? Quite simply, it's desire: the **desire to communicate**. Our need to get our message across gives us huge focus and sense of purpose; it's what engages us in the committed single-mindedness that plays a large part in making us compelling and real. In order that we can communicate with professional consistency and consistent professionalism, this desire is not discretionary. It's not a nice-to-have. You *have* to want to.

Just let those words sink in for a moment. You *have* to *want* to. Having to want to is quite a concept: it's a strange combination of obligation and choice. Having to want to is in itself a professional standard that will override all those sources of fickle, amateur energy we listed out in Chapter 4. An unwavering desire to communicate is a key source of performance energy and, as we've already seen, without performance energy you will come over as dull and flat, and wide open to all sorts of negative interpretation: people might see you as bored, tired, aloof, not bothered, slapdash... none of which is great for developing a relationship or advancing your career.

If the desire to communicate is key, **what happens if you *don't* want to?** What can you do to get yourself into the frame of mind where you *do*? For most people, the fear of exposure, the vulnerability of being the focus of attention, never entirely goes away. Whether we're making a major presentation or just asking a question in class, being in the spotlight with the **terror of humiliation** that almost always goes with it can either prevent us from speaking up at all or else seriously affect how we look and sound if we do. So how can we overcome such negative feelings in ourselves? Well, there are a number of motivational triggers you can use, but you need to find and focus on the one that works for you. This can be different at different times depending on how you feel.

Here they are:

Motivational triggers
Praise: short-term gratification
Reward: longer-term gratification
Audience: playing host
Fear/challenge

Let's look at these using simple examples...

Praise
Praise means 'I want a round of applause.' This could be actual applause, or immediate positive feedback after a meeting or interaction, e.g. 'Thank you, Alex, that was an interesting point you made/insight you gave.' You were visible, memorable. It takes much more than we realise to actually move anyone to give positive feedback spontaneously, so getting this sort of comment must mean you have made a serious impact!

Many of us don't feel comfortable with seeking praise as a motivation; we tend to feel that it is self-serving and somehow beneath us (the British, anyway). But if it serves the purpose of bringing all your motivational energy to the fore, if it unblocks your personal energy and gets the job done – use it! Seeking praise is a wonderful and fulfilling motivation, and can be very energising. You and your message have landed and everyone benefits – so don't be shy, get the praise.

Reward

Reward is a longer-term trigger. If you have to do something often, and are conscientious about doing it but find you are losing interest, then this may work for you: build in your reward.

It takes honesty and effort to make this one work. For example, Joe says to himself, 'If I make this work and do it *really* well, I'll take the afternoon off, have a gin and tonic, go and dig the garden.' Alex might say, 'If I do this really well I'll go shopping, buy myself a great pair of shoes or just go and play, get some friends together for lunch.' The key is to build in, up front, a reason for why you are going to reinvent what you're doing and energise yourself, by buying time to indulge yourself – and deserving it. This is called visualisation.

Audience: playing host

This comes relatively easily to extraverts, but also works well for the more introverted personality. It is often used as therapy for people who have a phobia or are crippled with shyness. One of the defaults of shy people is to feel that they are permanently the focus of scrutiny and judgement, regardless of whether that is the actual reality. One of the most useful exercises for them is to reverse the scrutiny and the exposure by turning it outwards – so that, in a communication sense, the focus comes *from* them and is all on the audience or other person.

Focusing on others' well-being as a motivation will turn a difficult or challenging situation on its head. We'll explore this psychology in the chapter on Transactional Analysis, but for now imagine you are giving a party, small or large. All your focus is on giving your guests a good time and making sure that they are happy and comfortable, and that they go away remembering the feeling of being well looked after and enjoying themselves. You can – you have to – forget about yourself and take care of *other people's* experience, through empathically focused expression – 'being with' the person. Consequently the focus is not on you.

The same applies in the context of presenting to an audience in a work situation. When you're next in a meeting or otherwise having to communicate with someone, experiment with thinking to yourself, 'I want you to feel comfortable and relaxed and have a good time, and I want you to feel good when I leave.'

This motivational trigger is often chosen by the high-level executives I work with, because it's a good fit with their status and takes the spotlight off them but at the same time leaves them with a strong role.

Fear/challenge

Now this last one is a bit of a teaser. How can fear possibly be a motivation? Well, it's more about *when* than why. Imagine this: you're bored, indifferent, preoccupied or unaware. So you walk into a meeting in one of these states: 'I'm not important enough to be here' or 'I'm too important' or 'There are other things I need to be doing.'

Red alert danger!

What this means in reality is that you are not properly present or 'in the moment', and that will show. Someone in that meeting will remember you afterwards, and that could have serious repercussions for your reputation and your future. It's like throwing a pebble into a pond; the splash ripples out and eventually reaches the bank. If the ripples are positive – 'That was an interesting point Alex made' or 'I must get a meeting in with Joe,' – then that obviously carries your reputation forwards and upwards; but if they're negative – 'Who? I don't remember anyone called Alex' or 'That guy Joe seemed distracted/only interested in himself/a bit quiet' – then as they spread far and wide the ripples can damage your reputation and career in all sorts of hidden ways.

In my career as a performer I found fear/challenge very effective. In a long or medium-length run the cast's collective performance energy can easily dip to a mediocre level. One very effective trigger for recharging this energy is if you think there might be someone in the audience who could impact your career. A rumour spreads: Steven Spielberg is in town and he may well be in the audience (he does this when he's putting a new film together). Or a powerful casting agent or agent for a big star has come to see the play (or any agent or casting person for that matter – keep it real!). This brings in a competitive edge that raises the energy and the game of the whole cast.

But you shouldn't focus on someone who you know for a fact will be watching the play (or, in a work context, who you know to be in your presentation audience); that's likely to put you under too much pressure and not be helpful. You need to stay in control of it, so keep it imaginary. Just remember – there will always be someone out there who might matter.

To recap, then, these triggers are all about getting you into the right mindset, motivating you to 'want to' and **releasing the energy** to make the effort. But what do you do if none of these triggers works, and you really do not want to?

Well, first of all, if you follow the directive of 'having to want to' and take it as an absolute given, I guarantee that you'll make some very clear choices. First, about your content, your 7% (remember the Communication Wheel?).

Let's say you've been asked to make a presentation, or put forward a particular argument in a meeting. Look at your content: does it make sense? Do you believe in it? Have you worked out what its impact might be? If your answer to at least the first two questions is No, then your options are to say, 'No, I won't do it,' or else, 'I'll only do it if I can find a way of making it powerfully my own.' Because if you don't or can't, this will seriously undermine the emotional energy you need in order to make you and your presentation 'land', and so make it almost impossible to energise others. A good example of this, to my mind, was Theresa May in the Brexit negotiations: in her heart she was a Remainer, but she had to sell 'Leave'. I feel she made it her own, as far as she was able, by re-engineering the execution of Brexit as a point of duty and responsibility to her country. But this wasn't enough to fuel the passion necessary to move hearts and minds.

Anything less than an authentic personal alignment to the content will mean blocked energy; and then you are left having to act it or fake it. As an actor, when landing a job – any job! – becomes your all-consuming objective, you find ways of dealing with these situations. In my early career, I occasionally found myself having to work with a second-rate script and make mediocre dialogue work. I remember doing a play and getting embroiled in a heated argument about the pronunciation of 'Tuileries Gardens' – 'Tooleries,' said the producer; 'Tweelerie,' insisted I. I went along with it to keep the peace and because the director begged me, but the line simply didn't work. Moral: if it doesn't work, have the courage to say no.

SUMMARY CHAPTER 9

• It's up to you to decide in which situations you want to communicate with optimum effectiveness. But it's important to make this decision intelligently from an aware and skilled place. Awareness brings choice; and choice brings confidence.

• To do it well, you *have to want to*. You need the desire to communicate. This is a vital element in releasing the flow of energy – your fuel.

• Use motivational triggers (ones that are in your control) to generate and focus your performance energy if the desire is lacking:
- Praise
- Reward
- Audience/host
- Fear/challenge

Things to work on
Make a note of the occasions when your desire to communicate flags, and try to work out why. Is there a pattern to these situations? Experiment with the various motivational triggers to find out which one(s) work best for you and where. And/or learn to start saying No more often.

CHAPTER 10

You In the 'Where' – Performing In Small, Medium and Large Arenas

'Space: the final frontier.'
Star Trek

We've already looked at some of the sources of our own personal energy (Chapter 4). What we're going to consider now is how space (the 'Where') impacts on us, and how it can influence our energy and desire to communicate in different situations. Unless we are aware and in control of it, the 'Where' can pull the rug from under us: it can make our energy and performance inconsistent, so that we actually look and sound different across different situations. This is detrimental to our brand.

Your objective is to transcend any negative, sabotaging feelings you may have by being able to perform yourself anywhere. This applies as much to the virtual world as it does to the 'physically present': different situations and audiences, which always vary in their size, type, configuration and responsiveness, require the same level of performance from you, regardless.

Alex and Joe are pitching together to a prospective client. Joe has prepared his 'content' and his argument in great detail and feels that he's got it just about right. Alex has also prepared, though not in such detail, but feels that she knows exactly how to articulate and express what she wants to get across.

They enter the meeting room, and this is what happens...

Alex sits down and engages fairly quickly and expressively with the six people round the table, building rapport (she has done her homework on who will be in the room), and is feeling fairly relaxed. Despite some natural nervous anticipation, her energy is released as she listens, asks questions, starts to describe her ideas. She knows that, given time, everyone will relax and join in, and a real conversation will start to happen. The people on the client side seem interested, intrigued even, and Alex is confident that she'll be able to bring the discussion to a harmonious conclusion with plenty of scope for continuation at a later date.

Joe on the other hand is quiet and says very little. He isn't very comfortable with 'close encounters', so his desire to communicate conversationally is limited and is inhibiting his energy flow – despite the fact that he believes passionately in what he has to say. He listens and observes and waits for his opportunity to contribute an interesting and well-thought-out point (he also has done some research into the company and its profile), but when he manages to speak he comes over as dry, with a monotonous voice and very little energy or impact. The people round the table struggle to engage with him or connect to his content (although knowing Joe it has been worked out in minute detail and would make absolute sense – if you were to sit alone in a room and read it quietly to yourself...).

While Alex is building relationships and having an impact Joe is not, and is fairly invisible at this point. The perception might be that he is aloof, indifferent, hard to read, detached, doesn't really want to be there... his presence in the room is rather confusing. Joe will have no relationship to progress from this meeting, and is likely to be quickly forgotten or remembered only vaguely or negatively.

But then, suddenly, the tables are turned. The lead on the client team asks Alex to start the formal part of the pitch. She is given a space to stand at the head of the table, and offered the use of a slide projector if she needs it. She picks up her notes and starts – and the 'downward drift' begins: she becomes wooden, nervous, low in energy, and her initial impact, engaging personality and natural conversational flow deflate gradually like an old party

balloon. Her message doesn't land, she doesn't land. The golden bullet (remember that from Chapter 5?) is fired from a rusty old blunderbuss.

Now it's Joe's turn. He stands and takes over from Alex. Suddenly the story makes sense; everyone sits and listens and is engaged, the message lands, he lands, the energy in the room is alive again.

The 'Where' – the space they are in – has revealed a fundamental difference between them. Can you work out what has happened, what the difference is? Well, the two of them are different types: Alex is essentially what I'd describe as a 'one-to-oner' and Joe is a 'closet performer' (I'll explain why 'closet' later).

Alex is clearly someone who is comfortable, unselfconscious and able in the small arena: she finds interactive and social situations (even formal ones) easy to manage; she's at home one-to-one or with about four to six people sitting round a table. But being 'out there' in front of people, on her own, closes her down and she loses her confidence and becomes self-conscious. Horrible! Terrifying!

Joe on the other hand is almost the reverse: he has the 'close-up' terrors. He finds being close up to people intrusive and worrying. He needs time, space and quiet to process, which is difficult 'in the moment' in a more personal and interactive situation; but put him 'out there', alone in front of people, and he is in his element because he'll have worked everything out in advance by putting in prep time, and he can apply structure and logic. And in the pitch meeting he has the freedom and space, without interruption and interference from the outside world, to communicate all those thoughts from inside his head that, usually, he isn't assertive, aware or confident enough to get out.

Now I'd like you to think about and write down the 'perception labels' that would be given to each of these types. I've given you a few suggestions in the table below to start you off. Remember that this is how we label people – by how we perceive them based on how they come over. Most of the time this is driven by a micro form of unconscious bias, and we do not stop to consider what is really driving someone's behaviour or our response, what is the reality behind what we see. Do any of these ring a bell? Add your own...

One-to-oner	Closet performer
Confident	Quiet
Gregarious	Reserved
Fun	Aloof
Out front	Cold
Motivating	'Hard to read'
Energising	Intimidating
Overwhelming	Authoritative
'Takes up all the air in the room'	Analytical
Exhausting	Clever
In your face	Thoughtful
Flaky	Has gravitas
Unconsidered (unreflective)	Considered (reflective)
Insensitive	Sensitive

Alex and Joe's experience at the pitch demonstrates that the 'Where' can have a big impact on how we perform, and consequently on the impression we make on people in different arenas. There are myriad factors that play into this equation, but there is one principal one, which we'll take a look at now.

Simply put – and as you've probably already worked out – Alex is an extravert, and Joe an introvert.

What does all of this mean in terms of communication? Broadly this: introverts are naturally more comfortable than extraverts in the large arena (and vice versa). If this seems counterintuitive, think about it in terms of where people get their energy from. The large arena is an 'alone' and unintrusive place that doesn't allow any interaction. It's when we're up on a platform or stage, with a clear space separating us from the audience. This space suits the introvert just fine: they don't need any external energy from the audience, and their inner energy makes them self-sufficient. Even better, the absence of any interaction means that they can perform without interruption, so there's nothing to derail their carefully worked-out argument or sequence of thought. It's here that an introvert, with the right understanding and performance skills, is predisposed to blossom and shine.

Now the extravert. Almost the exact opposite applies here. The extravert gets their energy from other people – so *needs* people. As an extravert myself, I know how difficult I can find it to marshal my thoughts into coherent articulation unless I can bounce them off someone else (very annoying for my husband – an introvert – who doesn't find the constant intrusion easy to live with, but is very patient). So the extravert will be the life and soul of the party down the pub or at a small gathering, and people can easily assume that they would be naturally brilliant as a speaker in any situation. But as we see with Alex, this is often far from the truth.

How I Define Arenas
What constitutes a small, medium and large arena is pretty subjective, and would be defined differently by different people. But for clarity, I describe them as follows:
Large
In my experience of coaching people, the large arena generally inspires the greatest fear, initially at least. A large arena is where we're alone in front of say 30 to 500 people.
Medium
Six to 30 people, maybe talking around a table, or in a workshop or seminar when you're standing at a flipchart. Medium arenas would also include social situations, a drinks party or dinner where you may have to 'say a few words', or a committee.
Small
When you're talking to or interacting at close quarters with 1–5 people.

Virtual communication platforms (Zoom etc) blur the boundaries, because we're accessing different sized audiences via a single point: the camera. This can lull us into a false sense of security, which is dangerous. The golden rules here are, first, perform *beyond* the camera (see Chapter 11); and second, if you don't feel there's a Cliff here … there is! Treat it with respect.

But, I hear you ask, what happened to Alex when she was standing at the head of the table? It wasn't exactly a 'large' arena, was it? Well, that opens up a fascinating quality of arenas: it's not necessarily their actual physical size that we find intimidating, but the feeling of exposure that they trigger inside us. Think back to that first piece you did to camera. Even if you were quite close up, I bet you felt exposed and vulnerable, and not like you were having a relaxed conversation with someone. (I appreciate you were talking to an inanimate object – the camera – and that you might argue that you'd feel more comfortable if there were people there. But in fact the feeling of exposure would still be the same). That's exactly the exposure that Alex felt when she made the apparently small move from sitting at the table to standing up, on show, a small distance from it. It was a small move in terms of physical distance, but clearly, for Alex, it was a big psychological jump.

In terms of physical space the difference between the small, medium and large arena can be minimal: what defines and differentiates them more are things that trigger psychological responses in us, such as the level of interaction with the other people present, a sustained focus on one person, a feeling of being judged... And these things happen in different places for different people, depending on their psychological profile – as we saw with Alex and Joe. In a similar way, how we use space can transform it from one type of arena into another. For example, I sometimes encourage my clients to stand up to speak in a meeting where convention would have them sitting down. The difference in their impact and the relationship between them and the audience can be huge.

I've often observed a mistake that companies make when casting people to go out front and represent them in formal situations – major presentations, conference speeches and the like. All too often they choose an extravert, because they are seen as gregarious, confident, outward going – the obvious choice. But when they're out there, cut off from their usual source of energy, the extravert can flounder badly. In a formal big arena, where there is no interaction with the audience, the extravert's usual energy supply is cut off, and they lack the introvert's inner energy to carry them through. Once the natural communication skill of the extravert becomes self-conscious the 'downward drift' starts to happen, or worse, they freeze (unless of course they're aware, know what to expect, have practised and prepared). By contrast, the introvert probably won't give off any clue that they might be good in these situations, because day-to-day they appear shy, retiring, quiet, internal. And they probably have no inkling themselves, either, that they might be good 'big arena' performers, because they find the prospect as intimidating as the next person – until they understand the dynamics and techniques of it, and have actually tried it. But when they do try it, and have gained a bit of experience, they often take to it like a duck to water. They come out of the closet (hence 'closet performer', like Joe).

Let's add this to the mix: which side do you think a lot of very good actors come from? Some are extraverts of course (and sometimes show-offs, like me!), but more often than not they're introverts. Sounds rather unlikely, doesn't it? How can that be? Well, in my nearly thirty years' experience of working with the amazing people I've known, I've observed that the introvert finds release in expressing the intensity of their inner life, and as an actor they are of course able to do this through performance. Indeed, if this intensity doesn't have an outlet it can lead to depression and isolation, so being an actor creates a balance. Additionally an introvert typically has a very rich inscape (that they draw on to inform the character they're playing), and a real need to find the balance. I always recommend that people who don't have this professional outlet join a group where self-expression plays an important part: team sport, amateur drama, singing in a choir, a book or poetry club where people read out loud… all help release that all-important fuel, performance energy, to create 'flow' and help you be happier in your skin. Repression is depression; expression is release.

Of course, in order to have your **You brand** you need to perform equally well in both the small and the large arena, and all points in between. (You can always switch off of course! You only have to be 'on' when you need to be present and contributing.)

How then does an extravert take their natural skills from the small to the large space? And how does the introvert do the reverse?

Well, simply put, with performance energy – and an awareness that whether you are introvert or extravert, performing 'you' is the same wherever you go. One space may feel more natural and easier than the other, so the skills for one will need to be more consciously learned. An extravert transferring their natural 'small arena' skills to the lonely big place – those formal situations where they feel cut off from their natural source of energy – will find it helpful to develop a conversational style and 'have a chat', even when no one is talking back: things like 'I'm sure we've all had the experience of…' or 'Is this ringing bells with you?' or 'What this means for you, Derek/Alice is...' – with real eye contact. This works well in smaller meetings but can be used to great effect in the large arena as well. All of this needs practice.

Conversely, an introvert needs to take their new-found freedom of expression from the big space to the small interactive arena, and realise that they have to be present, express and connect close up – and do this faster than feels natural, which needs conscious effort. Again, this takes practice; but if you're an introvert, it's likely that the more you do in the big space, the more your confidence will grow; and over time this will spill over and start to change how you think about, and perform in, the smaller, more interactive space. So you'll be well on the way to becoming a rounded communicator.

You get interesting dynamics between extraverts and introverts. Extraverts tend to speak things out to work them out, whereas introverts work things out then speak. So in meetings this can cause frustration on both sides: the extravert resents what they see as the silent uninvolvement of the introvert, while the introvert finds the extravert's relentless chat an intrusion on their thought process. And by the time the introvert has worked everything out and is ready to say something, the extravert has probably left the room to discuss it with someone else!

The Introvert–Extravert Scale

Here's an interesting exercise you might like to try. Draw up a simple scale, a line with extreme extravert at one end, and extreme introvert at the other:

E _____ I

Mark on it whereabouts on the scale you think you were before the age of twelve.

Now mark on it where you think this moved to after the age of twelve. Then where you are now; then where you would like to be.

Over time, the performance work that you are learning about in this book tends to move people towards the centre point, to becoming ambivert – a good balance between introvert and extravert. This isn't about abandoning your natural default place or feeling that there's anything wrong with it; but it's useful for everyone to work towards the middle of the scale and develop an ambivert facility, and not feel locked into one side or the other.

Here's a really crucial point to think about in all of this. When I start working with them, many of my clients say that they're 'naturally' good in certain situations but not others. From a professional performance perspective – which is what we're working on here – whether you're an introvert or extravert may be a reason that you respond differently, instinctively, to one arena compared with another. But it's not an excuse to do so. **Introversion and extraversion are just another source of subjective, amateur energy;** things to add to one side or the other of the 'What gives/takes away energy' list in Chapter 4. In performance terms, **whether you are an introvert or extravert makes no difference!** Performance energy and the discipline of the performance toolkit override these feelings and enable you to perform in all situations regardless of any default psychological disposition you may have.

It would be unthinkable, wouldn't it, for a professional actor to turn down a part because of the size of the theatre, or the level of intimacy it required, or to perform less well in certain roles on the grounds that they didn't feel comfortable because they were an introvert or extravert. Because of their professional training, **these considerations are a matter of complete indifference to the actor** when it comes to doing the job, and can simply be ignored. All they have to do is make the technical, physical and vocal adjustments required by the different arenas, and they can perform anywhere to the same level of excellence. What you are learning from this book will allow you to do the same. It's for this reason that I prefer the terms 'one-to-oner' and 'closet performer': they don't have the same psychologically 'set in stone' feel as extravert and introvert – they are things that can be worked on using the performance toolkit, overcoming weaknesses and capitalising on strengths.

The next exercise will help you to practise the adjustments you need to make in order to perform effectively in different arenas.

Exploring the continuum

I now want to look in more detail at our relationship to space and our emotional reactions to it, and the adjustments we need to make in order to manage different spaces and be effective in them, rather than just coping or avoiding them altogether.

We know that to have a consistent, reliable and genuine brand we must shine in all three arenas – small, medium and large – and that performance energy pulls it all together and transcends the emotional ups and downs that happen when we feel challenged (and unless we're prepared for it, the 'Where' can challenge us big time).

If you look back at the Journey Map, you'll see a list of adjustments we need to make when we move between different size arenas. They are:

- Physical
- Vocal
- Technical
- Strategic
- Emotional

Depending on who and where your audience is (whether two people or 500), you will need to address these adjustments – and do so fast and accurately. This ability will become part of your instinctive toolkit.

 I was playing Lady Macbeth for the British Actors Theatre Company (BATCO)... our first tour date was the prestigious Arundel Festival in Sussex. Nestling in the South Downs is Arundel Castle, the home of the Norfolks. We were to put on the play outside with the castle as backdrop. Picture the scene: dusk descending, the lights throwing eerie shadows on the castle walls, a thousand people sitting and lying on the grass. It was like a Greek amphitheatre. We had never had such a challenging arena. No microphones (no self-respecting actor uses a mic). It was clear to us that any real subtlety of expression was out of the question. How do you convey the richness, the layers of meaning that Shakespeare gives us in a big arena like this? Quite simply (not that it is simple) through clever adjustment and use of performance tools.

The next tour venue was a studio theatre in Peterborough. No more than 150 people in the audience, a small atmospheric space with plenty of scope for nuance and subtlety of meaning. In terms of adjustment, the skill here was not to lose your performance energy and go very quiet, yet not to stay on the same level as the big arena had demanded. The smaller space allowed us to be more intimate and intense, with greater subtlety and nuance; but landing such complex interpretation took just as much performance energy, if not more, than the bolder, bigger performance at the Castle.

The adjustments we need to make as we move from one arena to another are necessary to maintain the integrity of what we're saying and its meaning, and to allow its impact to be felt fully. In a large arena, this mainly comes down to using pause and emphasis (with plenty of performance energy) to dictate a slower pace and more space for the meaning to land as intended. Imagine you're throwing a large beach ball to someone at a distance and having it caught and thrown back: that's the time it takes for the purpose and intention of your words to carry and land with impact. Only 7% of the impact comes from the actual words themselves; 93% comes from how you throw them, wait for their return and catch them.

Performance energy is what allows you to simultaneously express and control emotion. As a good example of how performance energy and the Variety Pack help you make appropriate emotional (as well as vocal and physical) adjustments to the space you're in, think about delivering a tribute to someone you know and care about. It's very easy for the emotion to overwhelm and choke you, but breathing and using performance energy will allow the rich texture of your emotion to come through, and this is what really connects us to each other.

A CEO client rang me one afternoon with an anxious question: 'I have to give the personal tribute to my father at his funeral. How do I control the emotion and not become overwhelmed?' We can all identify with that, I'm sure. Feeling emotionally moved is a wonderful trigger and can transform our connection with the audience – but how can we use it, and avoid it using us? Quite simply by regarding it as fuel, because that's exactly what it is: Emotional Energy Expressed (think back to the Storywheel in Chapter 6). So I told him to use it rather than trying to sit on it. Later he phoned me again and said, 'Wow! It worked!' He sounded surprised; but his experience is at the heart of what you're learning in this book. And having to do it is the best way of learning and becoming confident in it.

Using performance energy and the performance toolkit helps us to express *out* rather than swallow our emotion. For many of us, trying to swallow and hide emotion is a natural reaction; but we need to practise working against this, because once performance energy becomes instinctive and we know how to control and let go at the same time, our emotion is our best friend.

Please now refer back to earlier in this chapter to remind yourself of the definitions of the small, medium and large arena. The next exercise – the Continuum – is about developing your ability to move seamlessly between the three sizes of arena, and doing them one after the other – in conversation, in a continuum – so that the process of 'contrast and compare' makes you very aware and familiar with the adjustments you need to make to perform well in each. Please read the following instructions through first before you start, so you understand how the exercise is put together – and remember, you can repeat it and work on specific parts of it as many times as you want.

 The Continuum Exercise
You'll need a large room, ideally around ten metres long (or else a corridor or back garden), two chairs, a friend and a camera. The friend is there to ask you questions to help you articulate and disclose around a situation or feeling that has acted as an obstacle to your confidence. This exercise is to help you articulate that, using the Variety Pack in different arenas (small, medium, large), but keeping the conversation going. As you move between the three spaces, take a moment in each to come out of the conversation and describe how you feel: 'I feel more/less comfortable, more/less free here...'

Throughout this exercise, the subject I want you to talk about is you. This is where we examine big time the power of personal disclosure. The question for your friend to ask you (or you to ask yourself) to get started is 'How do you *feel* about your dilemma/problem/challenge/situation?' Choose whatever is most pertinent to you right now. The objective here is to start expressing yourself, using the performance toolkit that you now understand in order to do this. Always use 'I', but from a position of truth, genuine reflection and authenticity. This exercise is meant as far as possible to be one long conversation.

To keep the explanation of the exercise as simple as possible, I'll assume you have a friend in the room with you. If you don't, just imagine that I or someone else is there (you'll need to ask yourself the questions. These need to be direct and really push you back).

The exercise starts in the small arena. Set up your camera so that you are centre frame. Remember to adjust the position of the camera as you move into the medium and then the large arena (or ask your friend to do this). Sit opposite your friend, fairly close up, and get them to ask you a question that will start your disclosure, e.g. 'Why are you finding this challenging/difficult/exciting etc?' or 'I get a sense that you're feeling blocked/frustrated at the moment. Is that true?'

Talk about this for two minutes or so, then get up from the chair and stand by it, so you're in a different space and you feel different. Carry on with the conversation for about thirty seconds then stop and register how you feel going from sitting to standing: does it open you up or close you down? Put you into 'flight' or 'freeze'? Do you feel more or less comfortable? Carry on talking, using 'all of yourself', as you slowly move backwards, always facing your friend's chair and the camera (which needs adjusting now to keep you in shot), and gradually 'upping' the performance energy to accommodate the need for more projection to cover the space, using plenty of pause and 'thinking' time. Let the energy travel down your arms through to your hands. Choose your words and meaning to land as you really want. When you're about 4–5 metres away from the camera, you have arrived in the 'medium' arena.

Take a pause. How does it feel here? Make a mental note. Now use your performance energy and the Variety Pack: louder/softer... faster/slower..., using pause and emphasis to modulate and your hands to reinforce what you're saying. You still have good scope for nuance and subtlety in your expression and meaning, though slightly less than in the small arena. You can keep an interactive, conversational style, even though you are not now actually in conversation but are out there on your own, with all the focus on you. Use plenty of pause and emphasis to bring meaning and life to what you need to 'land' and to include people in.

Move around, aligning your movement with your pauses and gestures, and look at one (imagined) face and then another; but keep the connection to everyone strong and focused. Remember, although you are not having real interaction with the audience – unless you actually do have someone in the room with you – keep it as chatty and normal as you can. Treat the camera as your friend.

See how this feels, and afterwards make a note in your **You brand** diary of how this particular space affects you.

Now move as far away from the camera as your room allows, up to around eight or ten metres. Welcome to the large arena! I think you'll find that the physical and vocal adjustments needed here are fairly self-evident: when you watch yourself back on camera, you'll see that in order to come across as normal you have to be louder, use bigger, more deliberate gestures, project more, with slower delivery and using a lot of pause and emphasis to land your words and their meaning. You'll find you need far fewer words, but that more meaning and clarity will come in the space around the words. You'll have more time to land key points and feelings. Your physicality should follow your intention: take your time and align your gestures with your speech pattern, giving time for your words to land and time for your audience to process for a few moments so that we 'get' it. You're still using disclosure, you're still using how you feel about things, and if you have your friend there they can ask you questions: 'Tell me more about that', 'Explain that to me', 'Describe that a little please.' It's all about you bringing yourself more and more to the fore and using your head, your heart and your physicality to bring it all together. Because that's when the 'flow' begins to happen, and you start to be in your body not just your head, and you are expressive and able.

Once again, here in the big space, take time out to check in on how you feel: 'Do I suddenly feel alive and freer, using more energy? Or am I utterly terrified? Do I feel very uncomfortable here?' Fine, take a note of it, it's all fine.

In order to make the adjustment to the big space, you may find it helpful here to throw an imaginary beach ball, speaking as you throw, then pause for the length of time it takes for the ball to be caught by the person you're talking to (ten metres away) and for them to throw it back. This will give you a good feel for what working in the big space demands. Remember: ***twice the energy and half the pace***. Use pause and emphasis to support this, with plenty of modulation and variety in your voice. What will happen is that you'll automatically start to edit out a lot of words, and what you say will become simpler and clearer. Magic! But there's also less room for subtlety: everything needs to be bigger, slightly exaggerated and larger than life in order to come over as real, normal and the 'right size' – pauses longer, messages bolder and more pronounced, more light and shade vocally and in terms of speed and pace.

Emotional connection

This is another very important aspect of our performance and one that the big arena brings out. You might at first struggle with emotional connection and find it confusing, because it can be quite unsettling. Emotional connection doesn't mean 'getting all emotional', bursting into tears or giving vent to a paroxysm of anger. It means just what it says: it's a state of being connected with our feelings (not just our thoughts) about whatever the subject is. Remember I keep saying that communication is a 'whole person' experience? Well, our emotions are a massively important integral part of that whole person, and our communication would be badly depleted and weakened if they weren't in the picture! They connect us to our message in a deeper way, and make that message clearer and bolder. Emotional connection is an essential part of our impact, and what makes us look and sound real, normal and natural. It's ownership.

Why the big arena brings out this connection to our emotions isn't exactly clear. But I've observed the process countless times and my intuition tells me that there's a direct correlation with the physicality of performance energy, which in a big arena has to be generated at a high level in order to fill the space. As it travels up from our gut, through our arms and out through our hands, face and body, the energy brings with it our deep-seated feelings and emotions, which can otherwise stay locked away and hidden. There's a reason we talk about 'gut feeling' – it's because that's where these emotions live. And that's part of the real magic of the performance process: it brings out parts of ourselves that we may have been oblivious to; it has the power to reveal us to ourselves.

The continuum and the 'I' statement

In this next part of the Continuum Exercise I want to help you capitalise on this power. Whilst at the back of the room, go to the wall nearest you and, facing it, place your hands flat against it at shoulder height; keep your feet firmly rooted and slightly more than hip distance apart; now *push* hard against the wall as though you were trying to get through to the other side. Ideally you will also have someone to push you from behind, so that this combined force travels right through your body, which acts as a conductor for the energy – but it will still work if you're doing it on your own.

Push as hard as you can, and as you push come up with an 'I' statement using disclosure, free from any self-conscious constraint. Imagine you're at the top of a mountain and can shout freely to the world something you might never say in everyday life, such as 'I want to be brave' or 'I need to break free' or maybe 'I feel stuck!' – anything that comes straight from the heart. This freedom of expression will come quite naturally when you are in a state of energised physical connection, because your head, heart and body will be brought together.

Do this several times until you are simply 'being' and expressing something that is meaningful to you. It won't work if you try to fake it. On the last practice, move away from the wall, stand up straight and turn and speak your statement to the camera with all your focus and energy – and revel in the freedom! The important thing is to be totally connected and free physically, and to make a real commitment to your statement. So no stuck hands or clenched fists; the energy must travel right through to your fingertips: have an open chest, use your arms and hands as energy conductors, then if the emotional connection and the intent are congruent your body will follow quite naturally. But you have to let it, and not repress it, as so often happens because we feel self-conscious about expressing our feelings. The key here is to stay centred and genuine. (Use your new self-awareness and the techniques you've learned to fight your instinctive terror of humiliation. Tell yourself it may feel risky – but it's riskless. You are a Formula 1 car.)

Using our physicality like this can work wonders in enabling us to break out of our inhibition. If you play any sort of sport you will know that, when you run out onto the pitch or sportsground, you have to use your physicality; you 'have to want to' if you're going to be any good; and your intent will literally drive the ball (or whatever it is you're playing with) – well, the communication 'ball' is no different.

So, having successfully and unselfconsciously expressed your 'want' to the world via the camera, now let that focused and powerful energy gradually bring you back to the 'small' arena – move back closer to the camera and discuss with it (or your friend) what significance this statement has for you: why do you want this? How do you feel about it? What does it mean to you?

It may feel risky – but it's a riskless risk. You are a Formula 1 car.

When managing the big space starts to flow and you feel properly engaged, are applying the 'Variety Pack' comfortably and feel 'in the zone' in terms of energy, feel your connectedness and start gradually to bring all of that back, through the medium space to the small, sitting back at the table as you continue in dialogue with a real or imagined person, all the while maintaining the same level of energy that you had to use in the big arena. Check you're in the 'ready for action' position (sitting upright, on your sitting bones, legs uncrossed, feet planted on the floor hip distance apart), using open body language and your hands to express and describe. Stay on your subject matter using the same energy as you did at the wall, so that you are bringing that unifying energy back from the large arena to the small. As you move back to the chair use the Variety Pack to adjust and modulate your performance appropriately as you pass through the different arenas. You will probably feel as you did in the 'Fred the Butterfly' exercise: out of your comfort zone! 'How can this possibly look normal and natural in this familiar, intimate space?' Please just feel the burn and do it anyway. After a minute or two, bring your 'conversation' to a conclusion, leaving us with a message, just like in the butterfly exercise.

Now play it back on your camera from the start of the exercise, all the way through. This has been an experiential exercise in travelling through the different arenas, exploring how you feel in them and what you have to do to be present and yourself in each one. You will see performance energy at work, acting like a glue to keep your head, heart and body together – *despite* where you are or how you feel. See where your **You brand** starts to come through; those places where you felt the most uncomfortable and self-conscious may be the very ones where you in fact look the best. That often happens: the places where we feel comfortable are usually within our comfort zone, and not where we perform most effectively. It's usually where we don't feel comfortable that we come out and start to grow hugely.

The three main things to take from this exercise are that:

• the skill of performing yourself is the same in all arenas. It isn't about being different in front of a large crowd from the way you are with just a few people or one-to-one. The authentic You, in your skin, is the same everywhere. There's no real difference between the large and the small arena; a slight adaptation perhaps, but essentially you have to inhabit yourself.

• where you are at your most effective may well be at the back of the room in the big arena, where you're probably most terrified – rather than where you feel most comfortable.

• you've made the connection between the big and the small arena, and see that moving between arenas just requires some fine-tuning rather than a radically different approach: more of or less of. Fundamentally all three arenas just require you to come out and express your authentic self in a whole person experience, head, heart and body.

Using performance energy makes everything fall into place seamlessly, no matter where you are or how you feel. Now you've seen your **You brand** in practice, and that by being truly connected you look and sound fabulous – the real you, at all times, looking and sounding normal, natural and engaging. This is a major breakthrough!

Take a break here, have a coffee and let the exercise settle – you might even leave it until tomorrow.

Then when you're ready...

 Review Everything So Far
Find your first piece to camera. Watch it through, and then watch everything you've filmed subsequently. See where **You** 'appear' and 'disappear'. The parts where you are really 'in the zone', using the Variety Pack and connecting emotionally using personal disclosure, are where you'll see yourself as being truly present, where your brand begins to shine through and have the authentic impact that, before, wasn't being seen or heard in the way you wanted.

This should give you real confidence to be 'more of you' and release the hero/ine within, the person you've always been but never quite realised: the leader, the partner, the influencer, the star – You! Free from the shackles of self-consciousness, and seeing exposure as a source of performance energy rather than terror.

After doing this exercise, write down in your **You brand** notebook the key lightbulb moments that you experienced, and all the things that suddenly made sense.

Kinaesthetics

I don't want to bog you down in too much theory, but I do want to introduce something here that you might like to play around with. In a theatrical context, kinaesthetics is the process by which actors choreograph their physicality, movement and performance through their relation to their position on the stage. Something like moving to a particular place on the stage or sitting in a chair will, through rehearsal, become associated with a particular line they have to deliver, an emotion they need to inhabit.

In terms of applying this to your performance of you in your everyday environment, try this exercise.

Statesman, Social, Intimate

Find the largest room you can. Imagine that it is divided into three sections. The back of the room is the 'statesman' space; the middle is the 'social' space; and the front of the room – nearest your audience, if you like – is the 'intimate' space. You will use each of these spaces to deliver a specific type of message, and you'll need to make adjustments to your physical, vocal and emotional energy as you move between the three of them.

Start at the back of the room, in the statesman space. Root yourself evenly on both feet, and don't move from this spot. Now deliver a big, statesmanlike, declamatory statement. For the purposes of this exercise, it's important not to get hung up on content, so I'll give you some: the nursery rhyme *Three Blind Mice*. Which goes like this:

Three blind mice, three blind mice
See how they run! See how they run!
They all ran after the farmer's wife,
Who cut off their tails with a carving knife!
Did you ever see such a thing in your life
As three blind mice?

Your opening, 'statesman' statement should be clear, bold and short, unemotional and just long enough to give the nub of what it is you're talking about without going into detail. Use the first line of the rhyme: 'Three blind mice, three blind mice'. Don't sing it, just use it as a piece of prose. Use a big open-armed gesture when you say this, without moving from your spot. Speak deliberately and with performance energy; take a breath and project it out, slowly and clearly. Decide which word you are going to put the emphasis on to give purpose, clarity and meaning (the meaning will change dramatically with your changes in emphasis – try putting it in turn on 'Three', 'blind' and 'mice' and see the difference it makes). Let the words hang. Don't rush on to the next thing but leave a pause and then repeat the statement a second time. Again, take the pause and let the words land.

Now walk forwards into the middle section of the room, the social space. Move quite quickly, but don't speak until you've arrived in the space. Then shift gear in terms of energy and tone. This is the place where you put flesh on the bones of your opening statement; so smile, speed up, move about, use gestures, tell anecdotes and paint pictures, use all the tools in the Variety Pack. This is the place to really connect with the audience and have some fun. Tell us some more about the mice: 'See how they run! See how they run!/They all ran after the farmer's wife/Who cut off their tails with a carving knife!'

You can change the meaning significantly by how you deliver the lines: you could be talking about some kind of Gothic horror, with a deranged woman slaughtering poor defenceless animals; or the totally justifiable eradication of loathsome vermin. (The rhyme is said to be an allegory for Bloody Queen Mary and the Oxford Martyrs.)

As a rule of thumb, stand still to deliver the really important bits: stand and deliver! Get into your skin and use your physicality as part of the vehicle for your message. Otherwise, you can move your feet; but don't bury your meaning under random, distracting movement; move with intent. If your head and your heart are connected, your body will follow your intent – let it.

Then stop talking, and move forward into the intimate space. Come to a standstill, take the pause. Draw the attention in to you by not speaking and being still. Then in a quieter voice – almost a whisper if you like; play around with it for effect – leave us with your 'ask'. This is your appeal, closing message or question to each individual member of the audience, the one thing you want them to take away when they leave. 'Did you ever see such a thing in your life/As three blind mice?'

Let it hang. Stop. (When you're doing this for real, it's very powerful to use an 'I' statement here.)

Kinaesthetics is a powerful tool for keeping your message structured, clear and impactful, but you will have to work hard at it. A professional actor gets masses of support – among other things, we are given a script that has been written by a professional, so it works 'out of the mouth'; we're given direction around where and how to move, and what to say where. But in your everyday life it's very unlikely that you'll get any of that. You have to do it all for yourself: you have to work out what you're going to say, how you're going to say it, how it needs to land and then how to choreograph your movement and timing.

Kinaesthetics isn't just limited to working in a big space. You can apply it to a meeting where you're sitting at a desk or table – for example, leaning back can put you into the statesman space, and forward into intimate. But you don't even have to move at all. You can differentiate between the three spaces just by using the Variety Pack of volume, pace, tone of voice, pause and emphasis – as well as your actual words – to keep a clear structure in what you're saying and signpost this to your audience.

To finish off 'You in the Where' we need to bring it all together and practise. So I'd like you to put together and perform three to four minutes on your experience of this last exercise.

 Have your Storywheel in front of you and, with a Beginning–Middle–End structure, work out your theme using personal disclosure (an 'I' statement using your own experience and feelings) to create the fuel to narrate the plot of your experience. So maybe 'Today I felt a little confused/anxious/excited/challenged by the next part of the journey, but...'. Remember to *describe* feelings and revelations using examples, anecdotes, 'for instances' – anything to paint the picture and create images that engage and connect, and allow us to literally see your meaning. Remember: twice the energy you feel comfortable with from a standing start, and *half* the pace. Put your pontoons – your right-brain triggers – somewhere you can just see them; you almost certainly won't need them (as you use them more, you'll find that pontoons and the process of working them out create neural pathways for your memory and become merely reassurance).

Do your piece to the camera, standing and moving in harmony with your meaning and expression (no distracting 'bleeding' energy or movement). Stand at least three or four metres from the camera and check that the screen can accommodate your performance area. Where the energy dips, or where pause and emphasis have got lost so the clarity of meaning and your intention are failing to land, do it again! And enjoy it!

SUMMARY CHAPTER 10

• The 'Where' (the arena we're in) can have a detrimental impact on our performance – unless we're aware and in control of it.

• Everyone sits naturally somewhere on the spectrum between 'one-to-oner' and 'closet performer'. Thinking in these terms helps release you performance-wise from the psychological straitjacket of 'introvert' and 'extravert', and work towards ambivert.

• Different arenas require you to make adjustments (physical, vocal, technical, strategic and emotional) in order to continue appearing real and natural in each one. This is key to your You brand.

• Despite the differences between arenas, you need the same performance energy and performance toolkit in all of them.

• Working in the large arena will help you find emotional connection with what you are saying.

• Kinaesthetics will help you choreograph your performance and ensure you and your messages land in the right way.

• Golden rule: twice the energy, half the pace! Use pause and emphasis to modulate.

Things to work on
There is a lot to take from this chapter. But a key thing I'd urge you to focus on is to monitor and work on your energy level in the different arenas you find yourself in. If you're in a small meeting, for example, be aware that you need the same level of performance energy (intent, focus and commitment) – adjusted for volume, size of gesture and so on – as you would use in a large presentation space.

CHAPTER 11

The Virtual World and Performing Into the Void

'We become aware of the void as we fill it.'
Antonio Porchia

The change in the world of communication brought about by our increasing dependence on the internet received a huge boot up the backside when the 2020 Covid 19 pandemic hit the world.

When I started writing this book the 'arenas' of personal communication were fairly clear: at work, the conference platform, boardroom, office, meeting room, media studio etc, and then all the myriad interactions that take place in our everyday lives, through relationships and community living. But suddenly we were catapulted into the communication 'void', and we had to get to grips with Zoom, Microsoft Teams, Webex, Skype, WhatsApp and the rest, things that we'd possibly only dabbled in before.

Oh my goodness, what a technology nightmare for most of us! At one and the same time we became more and less available to each other. The reality of being locked down with very limited physical access to human beings meant that we started to crave connection ... and lo and behold, riding over the plain to our rescue came the virtual communication platforms together with the devices (phones, tablets, laptops etc) to keep us in a suspended state of almost real time. Weird and wonderful all at once.

All of this quickly became a new 'somewhere' to master in the Confident Anywhere paradigm of this book. Quite literally, another platform that we must become good and professional on. So what does good look like here?

In the chapter title I refer to Performing into the Void. To clarify what I mean by this, it's helpful to recap the main argument of the book, which should by now be familiar ...

Actors learn to create an authentic reality and emotional congruence that allow us to believe in the character they are playing. In the same way, you can learn to perform the role of You, so that you too are believable, recognisable, consistent and reliable. Doing this requires you to be self-sufficient in how you use and deal with your fear, anxiety and nerves. You'll know by now that as a really confident professional performer of You there is no room for negative energy, which can easily close you down and leave you looking and feeling less than in control (look back at Chapter 4 to remind yourself of the difference between 'amateur' and 'professional' communication). Having the awareness and the skill not to be thrown by a negative internal script means you're not dependent on your audience for approval or a favourable response, for your energy.

All of this you know. So how does it relate to telepresence and 'performing into the void'? Well, we are *always* performing into an unresponsive space that is potentially negative – until we understand how it works and how to be in control. This new virtual arena simply makes manifest what is always there. I've often had clients say at the beginning of their first session, when I ask them to talk to the camera about themselves and their job: "Yes but of course this isn't natural; in real life I wouldn't be talking to a camera, so you're not going to see me as I usually am." But, as you'll have experienced when you did your first piece to camera, the experience of talking to an inanimate object is a pretty good simulation of what it's like to be out in front of an audience, whether it's three people or five hundred.

And now, talking to a camera isn't just a proxy for real life – it *is* real life. At least a part of it. Filming themselves for You Tube and other social media platforms is a central part of many people's real-life profiles, just as being interviewed by a camera is now commonplace in job interviews. For many people, using virtual platforms like Zoom and MS Teams now takes up as much of our time as physically present, face-to-face interactions used to.

Like it or not, these virtual platforms are here to stay. It's unlikely they'll ever replace face-to-face interactions and meetings entirely, but they will almost certainly continue to be a big part of our daily lives – certainly for business – even when the Covid 19 crisis has passed.

The way we come across in this arena will become an important determinant of our profile, reputation, success … indeed our

Our telepresence
will become a
key source
of competitive
advantage.

enjoyment of life. Our 'telepresence' and ability to use these platforms in a professional manner will become a key source of competitive advantage, both personally and for any organisation we work in. They will be a big part of the mix in how we develop and maintain strong relationships with colleagues and clients, run assignments, negotiate deals, win pitches and beauty parades, and deliver results. But also, virtual drinks, dinner parties, club meetings, choirs, music, theatre and countless other aspects of people's everyday lives have found a new form and a wider reach than ever before, and some of these are bound to continue after the pandemic.

Of one thing though I'm absolutely certain … all the awareness and techniques you've been learning about in this book are as relevant to this virtual arena as they are to any other. Performing effectively into a camera (which, it goes without saying, is a central part of the professional actor's craft, and was my job for many years) is not much different from performing into the void of 'real' life, whether it's to a large audience of blank faces, a meeting where no one gives you a clue as to what they think or feel about you, or even a difficult conversation where you've had to go out on a limb and are feeling exposed. So, just like the film actor or TV presenter talking to a character or audience that isn't there, the key to performing into the void is to talk to the camera like it's your friend.

'You're talking to one person. Use the camera as a best friend, not as an audience. Relax into it. You're just talking to your best mate, that's all. You like him and he likes you and he's ready to listen to every word you've got to say, he's very interested in you.'
Michael Caine

What follows is a practical guide to how to come over at your best in the virtual world. These notes focus on the performative aspects of telepresence, rather than the technical. They're not about which button to press to do what.

Alex is going to help. I hope you find it useful!

Position your device
Ensure that the camera on your device is at eye level.

This is important because …
There is a widespread (and natural) tendency to put your laptop, tablet, phone etc on the table in front of you and talk down at it.

This may be easy for you, but it doesn't create a good impression on the other person.

• The person you're talking to sees a lot of your ceiling.
• They feel like they're lying down and you're looming over them – this can be intimidating and interpreted in all sorts of negative ways (domineering, bullying, aloof etc).

LOOMING

• They'll probably be looking up your nose, and you're likely to sprout some extra chins. Not great, unless that's the look you're after …
• And if you sit with your laptop on your lap you'll present some even weirder angles and probably look wobbly as well.

NO

The Complete Works

YES!

So … prop your device up on some books: this will help create a normal perspective, and the other person will feel they're talking to you as if you were sitting across a table together.

If you want to be posh, instead of using books, there are some great stands for laptops that do the job much better. Google 'laptop lifts'.

Make sure you have the main source of **light** (window, electric light) in front of you not behind. Natural light is best.

LIT FROM BEHIND

Ensure the light is as even as possible on both sides of your face. If you usually Zoom from the same place you may want to buy in some lighting to balance and even out the natural light – you can get some excellent 'ring' lights these days, even mini ones that clip to your phone or laptop when you're on the move. Some have flexi arms to hold your phone or tablet.

Sit about 3 feet away from the camera on your device.

Show the top half of your body. If you are just a talking head you will be 'in people's face', and your physicality will be limited: you won't be able to use gesture to support your performance and make you look more natural and engaged.

Make sure though we can see more than just your fingertips popping up from the bottom of the screen; disembodied hands look weird.

Keep your **background** uncluttered, and a reflection of who you are. Personally, I don't like using the virtual backgrounds available on some platforms; they tend to 'flair' and make bits of you disappear.

Experiment with all of this until you find the look that you like.

Make eye contact
The camera on your device will never be in line with the eyes of the person you're talking to. So if you look at their eyes on the screen, they'll think you're looking somewhere else.

You think you're making eye contact – but you're not

People can interpret this in all sorts of different ways. They might think you look shifty. Or preoccupied. Or uninterested. Not really what you want, is it?

You get some of the worst cases of this when people use a tablet in landscape position – because the difference between eye - and camera-line is greater than with a laptop.

So to make eye contact, look directly into the camera. Tuck your chin in slightly to avoid looking down your nose:

Making eye contact on Zoom etc is counterintuitive, and can be tiring. Your focus is split between looking into the camera and looking at the person.

But remember: the impact you're making is the important thing. A headache probably means you're doing it right! Do go a bit easy on yourself though: aim for around 50% direct eye contact to strike a balance between sustainability and making it real.

Landing your message

While eye contact is important, it's also important to pick up on the non-verbal messages the other person is putting out.

So here's a technique for doing just that – and it's one that'll give you more impact into the bargain.

When you need to really land a point, try this: emphasise the preceding word or phrase, pause, lean into the camera slightly and look directly into it, give your important message, pause again, then lean back into your neutral position.

This will give real visual and vocal emphasis to the point you want to make. It also buys you some time off: you can relax eye contact for a bit, and look at the other person to read their response.

How to sit

Avoid slouching, crossing your arms, crossing your feet, and all the other things that may make you feel comfortable – but which may be giving off negative messages to the other person (uninterested, arrogant, defensive, unreceptive etc). Even if we can't see all of you, your posture will impact how you feel and how you come across.

I know we've already covered this, but here again are the notes on how to sit …

Sit with about 18" between navel and table. This gives you performance space and allows you to bring your hands into play. It stops you getting 'locked on' to the table, which looks uncomfortable, closed and defensive.

Sit up in the chair: sit on your sitting bones with your spine straight (feel how it immediately changes your energy, let alone transforming how you look?), pelvis tilted slightly forward, ear over shoulder – imagine there's a thread pulling up from the crown of your head – but stay relaxed, don't stiffen up.

Plant your legs about hip distance apart, your feet flat on the floor, hands resting lightly and openly on your thighs or lap. This is called the 'neutral' or 'ready for action' position. It may feel weird to start with, but it will soon transform how you look and feel.

Now you are physically taking more active ownership of your space and have more authority. And your body will like it.

Energise your performance
Just as with 'physically present' situations, you need to use more energy than you think in order to appear natural and normal.

To energise yourself, stand up, walk about, speak out loud (imagine you're talking to someone some distance away from you), use gesture, smile ... then sit back down at your screen, bringing all this energy with you. And maintain it throughout your meeting.

Perform *beyond* the camera. Remember that your audience is on the other side of it. If you treat the camera lens as your audience you'll stop there, and you won't reach people as powerfully as you need.

And remember to ...

Take breaks!
Using these platforms is pretty focused and intense, yet it doesn't give us the same energy feedback we get when other people are physically present. So every now and then – at least once an hour – take a break for a few minutes. It's best to agree this at the start of the meeting, so people can relax about it and pace themselves.

How to Listen
• Stay silent when someone else is speaking. Best to mute when you're not speaking.
• Maintain a good level of eye contact (look at the camera), but don't stare too intently as this can make you look blank and unresponsive, zoned out.
• Smile and nod to show agreement, or just that you're listening.
• It's important to show that you're listening, not just to listen.

Better with the camera off?
Switching your camera off is like turning up to a 'normal' meeting with a bag on your head. It's your choice – but think about the impact it has.

Overall
Remember, it's not about your comfort! Looking good and performing well in this virtual environment probably won't feel comfortable or natural, until you get used to it.

There will be times when you may feel like you're performing into the void, in that you're not getting much response from your audience (especially if there are a lot of people involved). Don't be put off by this. They may well be having a great time, even if they're not showing it. Remember: don't tune in to the energy level of the other people. Set the energy level that you know works.

Things to work on
In all of this, the best way of finding out what works for you is trial and error. So find a friend to practise with, and to make sure that what you think is happening matches what people on the other side of the screen are actually getting.

CHAPTER 12

You with the 'Who': Interacting With People – and with Yourself

'You don't get a second chance to make a first impression.'
Anon.

So far we've been looking at how you come across and 'occur' to others, and working on your self-awareness, emotional connection and the performance toolkit so that you always appear real and natural as *you*. Now we're going to turn our attention to an essential part of your **You brand**: how you communicate when you are *interacting* with other people.

Conversations and meetings – just as much as set-piece presentations and the like – form a large part of the way we are perceived by other people, so it's important that we maintain consistency in the way we behave in these situations. Obviously. But how often do we come away thinking, 'Damn! I wish I had/hadn't said that, reacted in such and such a way'? How often do we wish we could wind the clock back and start again? Why is it that we can feel so out of control, no matter how hard we try or how determined we are when we go in? The model I'm about to describe is a brilliant way of helping us to find our way through this psychological minefield and making these situations work for us, not against us.

Let's start with this...

If I wag my finger at you and talk in an angry voice, what happens to you?

You might feel nervous, frightened, defensive, guilty, on the back foot, like you've done something wrong... How do you behave? You might cower away, or cross your arms in self-defence.

And how do you feel in terms of being able to respond to me in a balanced, constructive way? Probably not great. If you were in an important conversation or negotiation, would all this make you feel good, confident, put you in a strong position? Almost certainly not. And even if you *felt* basically OK when faced with my finger-wagging, how did you *look*? Probably pretty startled, cowed and defensive – or maybe aggressive – any of which is likely to provoke a negative feeling in me about you.

But what is the reality here? Have you *really* done something terribly wrong? No, you haven't – at least, not as far as I know. What is it then that made you respond in that way? How can we make sense of all this, how can we deal with this sort of 'psychological slap' and not let ourselves be sabotaged by it?

Help is at hand – in the shape of something called Transactional Analysis, or TA for short. TA is a theory of personality, behaviour and communication. Drawing on the work of Freud, it was originated in the 1950s by Eric Berne, a psychiatrist and psychoanalyst. TA provides a framework for understanding what might be going on 'inside somebody' (or inside us) and how this translates into positive or negative consequences for their interactions and relationships with others.

What would TA say about our little finger-wagging exchange?

There's a Child – and a Parent – in all of us
A central idea in Transactional Analysis is that of 'ego states'. You'll find, with a bit of practice, that these can be very helpful in understanding what's going on in interactions between people. To help you grasp the concept of ego states, I'd like you to imagine that our interaction took place between members of a family living together in a house (the house is my model, by the way, not Berne's).

This house is made up of a number of rooms. At the top, in the attic, live the Parents, those wise people who always know best; but who, when they're in a difficult mood, can get pretty nasty, wagging their fingers and telling people off – as we've just seen. And they often take it out on the poor Children, who live in the basement and only want to be noticed and approved of by the Parents – and who, when they get told off, can get very upset and cry, or else rebel and throw their toys out of the pram.

This type of Parent Berne labelled the 'Critical Parent'. Moreover, he added another label: 'Negative' – Critical Parent Negative or CP– . A CP– is an authority figure of the bullying, aggressive variety.

They can be snide, accusing, autocratic, fault-finding, dismissive – generally pretty undermining. Not the sort of Parent you want to get on the wrong side of!

What's the likely response from the basement? Well, the Child responds and adapts to the Parent's authority; they fall in with the rules – in a rather downtrodden, self-negating, over-compliant sort of way: 'poor little me' or 'victim'. And even if they don't immediately comply with them (they may go into a rebellious strop rather than crying or cowering), they at least recognise the Parent's power. This is what Berne terms the 'Adapted Child Negative' or AC– .

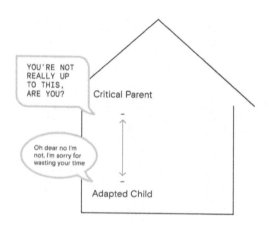

All pretty dysfunctional. But thankfully that's only one side of the relationship, one aspect of the personalities. Because there's also a *positive* side to Critical Parent ('Critical' in Berne's vocabulary, by the way, does not denote criticism in its purely negative sense, but means something more like a 'critique' – an assessment or judgement).

This 'Critical Parent Positive' (CP+) is the authority figure who sets limits and creates boundaries, who judges, disciplines, who makes and enforces rules – but in a constructive, positive way. They are clear, firm, reasonable and organising. A CP+ would come out with comments like 'There are certain rules that I really want you to follow, because they're there to keep all of us safe' (always wear your seatbelt; wash your hands on a hospital visit; abide by the rules and values of a company's culture); or 'If you ask for something, people generally respond better if you say please.'

In the same way, down in the basement, cheek by jowl with the Adapted Child Negative (pouting and cowering, or resentful, cross and rebellious, depending) is the Adapted Child Positive, or AC+. The motivation of AC+ is common-sense compliance; being law-abiding and cooperative. If the Critical Parent were to say, 'Please don't play with those scissors because they are very sharp and you might hurt yourself,' the Adapted Child Positive's response would be to say, 'OK, I won't,' and put the scissors down – or ask why.

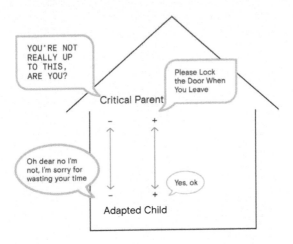

Now you'll have figured out that these aren't real people, but allegorical ones. They represent different 'ego states' and they can exist between different individuals as well as within one person. These ego states are psychological places that we all inhabit, and Berne's theory is that they are what drive interactions between people (there's a load of other houses on the estate!).

It's very important to emphasise that not only do the ego states influence our interactions with other people, but **also drive our interaction with *ourselves*.** We all run our own internal 'scripts'; we can all go into Critical Parent and Adapted Child on our own, without anyone else even being there. For example, you may go into a meeting running a CP– script in your head that says: 'I really shouldn't be here, these people are far more experienced and senior than I am, what on Earth was I thinking?', which will probably make you sit there in negative Adapted Child, not daring to say a word, going red and spluttering if someone asks you something – or else being overly accommodating, or perhaps confrontational and aggressive in an attempt to compensate. We'll look at strategies and techniques for dealing with these feelings in a moment; but simply being *aware* of what is happening inside you and seeing it in a more balanced perspective is a great place to start.

Let's fill in the rest of the rooms in the House...

In the other attic is another Parent: the Nurturing Parent. Again, this ego state has two aspects, positive and negative. The Nurturing Parent takes care of people, protects and nurtures. When it is positive, it is compassionate, reassuring and comforting – but also encouraging, enabling, supportive and releasing, helping people to discover their talents, do new things, take a risk and realise their potential: 'Yes you can!'

But when it's negative, Nurturing Parent can be controlling, smothering, invasive, overprotective, suffocating, debilitating: 'Don't you worry your little head about that, it's a bit beyond you, isn't it, leave it to me, I'll take care of it for you.' This can of course be very seductive, because it absolves us of responsibility: 'Goodie, I don't have to worry.'

In the other basement is our Free Child. The positive Free Child (FC+) is creative, spontaneous, curious, playful, doing no harm to itself or anyone else. But the Free Child's negative side is self-obsessed, reckless, irresponsible, egocentric and wild. It can act inappropriately, in an inconsiderate, un-boundaried or weak way:

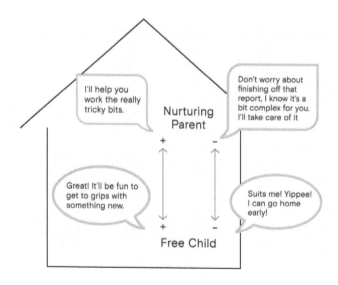

'Wayhay! Stuff the rules, let's party! Mum and Dad will make sure everything's OK; I don't have to take care of anything, I can do what I like.'

Where do these ego states come from?

The **Parent** state comes from our own parents or other authority figures who influenced us in our childhood. These are the people who passed on to us, through what they said and the way they behaved, a set of rules, ways of thinking and behaving: 'values' (or injunctions) to guide us through life. Things like 'All good things come to those who wait,' 'Money doesn't buy happiness,' 'Never trust anyone with dirty shoes,' 'You're special,' 'Always speak your mind,' 'It's rude to interrupt,' 'Don't show off,' 'Don't talk with your mouth full,' 'Family hold back,' 'Nice girls don't' (my mum), 'I just want you to be happy' (no pressure there then)... Positive, negative or indifferent, these injunctions exert a strong influence on us and many people never question them (or are even aware of them), accepting them as 'just the way things are'. This is the 'Taught' part of our make-up.

The **Child** ego state is the way we were as young children: emotionally connected, both needy and dependent and at the same time uninhibited, spontaneous and free. It's where our emotions reside, where we feel excited, fearful, happy, sad, needy, vulnerable. It is our 'Felt' place, our creative self.

Both of these states remain a part of us for life. They're not something we grow out of or into; they exert an influence on us always, they form part of who we are.

But one ego state is missing. **Adult**. The Adult lives in the sitting room, and regulates between our Parent in the attic and Child in the basement. There aren't two sides (+ and −) to the Adult; it's one whole (although see the box below).

Adult is the place where we have cut loose from the injunctions of our Parent, and have examined the feelings of our Child, challenged them and worked them through. Once we've done that, we can arrive at a personal and responsible place of real choice, which we can stick to even when we're under siege or attack. It's the place where we are truly and independently ourselves. It's where successful and safe interaction and negotiation happen (whether or not there's a final resolution) because there is no emotional or psychological (self-)sabotage or slaps.

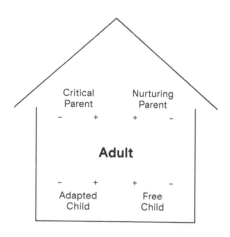

Although there isn't a positive and negative Adult state, there is a state of extreme Adult, which lies higher than neutral on the autistic spectrum. There's a lot of this at a certain level in business, because people have often been rewarded and promoted on the basis of their technical ability rather than their capacity for empathy or interpersonal skills. This may not serve them well when they reach a leadership role where they need the emotional intelligence to deal effectively with people and the ability to make creative leaps to grow the business. Here's an equation I often show clients, which helps put this in perspective:

$$\text{Human potential} = EQ(IQ + TQ)$$

Where EQ = emotional quotient, IQ = intelligence quotient and TQ = technical quotient. What the equation means is that the value of IQ and TQ is limited unless it is leveraged by EQ. In other words, you can be as bright and techie as anything, but without the multiplier of EQ you won't make the most of what you've got.

What's all this got to do with You brand?
Why, I hear you ask, are we going down this track, where there are so many possible battles to fight? Well, we're here because the relevance of all this to **You brand** is *huge*.

The ego states we inhabit determine the behaviour we manifest: how we look (physical appearance, facial expression, body language) and sound (tone of voice). They're a big influence on how we feel about ourselves and others, and how people see us and feel about us. It's not strictly accurate to say that there's a particular 'look' and 'sound' associated with each of the different ego states, because these vary from person to person. How we look and sound in our Child states, for example, derives from how we looked and sounded when we were *actually* a child, and this will be unique to each one of us.

However, in my experience, it is possible to generalise with a reasonable degree of accuracy. Here is a table of some of the common features and manifestations of each of the states – but it's best to use this as a guide for your own observations, rather than as gospel. As well as how we look and sound, it includes the words we might use and how we might be interpreted in each of the ego states.

Critical Parent Negative (CP–)

WORDS	GESTURES/ BODY LANGUAGE	TONE OF VOICE	FACIAL EXPRESSION	POSSIBLE INTERPRETATIONS
You must always...	Pointing finger	Sneering	Scowl	Patronising
	Hands on hips	Condescending	Frown	Condescending
Make sure you...	Looking down nose	Deep	Hostile	Judgemental
		Resonant	Disapproving	Concerned
How could you be so stupid as to...	Steepled fingers	Harsh	Corners of mouth pulled down slightly	Strict
	Shaking head			Disgusted
It's dangerous to...	Thumping desk	Drops at end of sentence	Eyebrows raised or drawn together	Over-responsible
We've got certain standards round here	Linking hands behind head	Cold		Stressed
		Flat	Tense facial muscles	Anxious
	Chopping air with hand	Arrogant tone		
Should	Leaning back in chair	Laughing at	Smiling only with mouth	
Ought		Derogatory	Intense	
Don't	Tilting head back	Patronising	Manic	
Must	Biting lip	Intimidating silence		
	Arms folded tightly across chest			

Critical Parent Positive (CP+)

WORDS	GESTURES/ BODY LANGUAGE	TONE OF VOICE	FACIAL EXPRESSION	POSSIBLE INTERPRETATIONS
You may find it helpful to…	Relaxed	Interested	Direct eye contact	Reassuring
	Warm	Warm cadence		Relaxed
Have you tried…?	Inclusive hands	Level tone but authoritative, giving clear direction	Nodding	Non-combative
Have you considered the impact this may have on other people?	Open body		Smiling with eyes and mouth	Firm
	Alert			Clear
	Positive			

Nurturing Parent Negative (NP–)

WORDS	GESTURES/ BODY LANGUAGE	TONE OF VOICE	FACIAL EXPRESSION	POSSIBLE INTERPRETATIONS
I'll take care of it for you	Pat on the head	Condescending	Affected smile	Comforting
	Smothering hug	Patronising	Looking down	Making excuses or allowances
Wrap up warm		Long-suffering sigh	Tapping foot	Suffocating
		Blank look		Closing down

Nurturing Parent Positive (NP+)

WORDS	GESTURES/ BODY LANGUAGE	TONE OF VOICE	FACIAL EXPRESSION	POSSIBLE INTERPRETATIONS
You can do this – I'll help you get started	Pat on the back	Encouraging	Relaxed	Trusted
	Open arms	Concerned	Warm	Empowering
Don't worry, better luck next time	Embracing	Patient energy in voice	Smiling	Allows choice
	Physically centred	Warm	Interested	Supportive
Well done!		Excited	Listening	Enabling
		Interested	Reflective	Energy giver
		Slow	Nodding	
		Listening		

Adult

WORDS	GESTURES/ BODY LANGUAGE	TONE OF VOICE	FACIAL EXPRESSION	POSSIBLE INTERPRETATIONS
What?	Open	Calm	Listening	Self-responsible
Why?	Thoughtful	Clear	Steady eye contact	Interested
When?	Precise	Even	Thoughtful	Detached
How?	Upright	Confident	Alert eyes	Evaluative
Is it practical?	Relaxed	Matter-of-fact	Reflective	Decisive
What is the logic?	Confident	Emotionally detached	Warm	Confident
Yes. No.	Calm	Decisive	Nodding	Independent
	Still			

Adapted Child Negative (AC–)

WORDS	GESTURES/ BODY LANGUAGE	TONE OF VOICE	FACIAL EXPRESSION	POSSIBLE INTERPRETATIONS
Please let me	Crestfallen	Whining	Fearful	Whiny
I won't!	Slumped	Sulking	Pouting	Placating
Why me again?	Hunched	Defiant	Blushing	Defiant
Can't	Cowering	Muttering	Frown	Petulant
	Vigorous head-nodding	Quiet	Looks out from under raised eyebrows	Passive aggressive
	Chin forward	Quavering		Childish
	Dejected			
	Nail-biting			
	Head on one side			

Adapted Child Positive (AC+)

WORDS	GESTURES/ BODY LANGUAGE	TONE OF VOICE	FACIAL EXPRESSION	POSSIBLE INTERPRETATIONS
I understand	Upright	Enthusiastic	Nodding	Sensible
That's fair	Relaxed	Calm	Clear eye contact	Supportive
I feel safe	Attentive	Level	Listening	Reasonable
What can I do to help?				Receptive

Free Child Negative (FC-)

WORDS	GESTURES/ BODY LANGUAGE	TONE OF VOICE	FACIAL EXPRESSION	POSSIBLE INTERPRETATIONS
I want!	Noisy crying	Loud	Manic	Reckless
What the heck!	Animated	Breathless	Staring	Dangerous
Who cares?	Frenetic	Excited	Grinning	Brash
Not my problem!	Demanding			Unrestrained

Free Child Positive (FC+)

WORDS	GESTURES/ BODY LANGUAGE	TONE OF VOICE	FACIAL EXPRESSION	POSSIBLE INTERPRETATIONS
That's fun!	Laughing with	Loud	Joyful	Spontaneous
Why not...?	Energetic	Free	Twinkling eyes	Relaxed
Let's...	Loose-limbed	Vital	Relaxed	Changeable
Sounds great!	Excited	Breathing freely	Animated	Unrestrained
That's exciting!	Funny		Warm	Impulsive
	Harmonious			Creative
				Inspirational

There's a great game to be had with this table: spot the ego state! I found you can get really hooked, as you go about your day, on observing people and trying to work out which of the ego states they're in, just from looking at them and hearing them – and observing yourself in response to others and their response to you. Then, if you want to add another level of complexity, look at whether there's any difference between *what* they're saying, the words they use, and how they look and sound when they're saying it (remember the Communication Wheel). But beware: behavioural clues are not a guaranteed indicator of ego state. A manipulative Adapted Child Negative can look and sound very much like a reflective Adult.

The table also raises some important questions:

What is the most important indicator of ego state?
Is it what we say, how we look or how we sound?

Berne distinguishes between two levels of interaction: social and psychological. The social level is about the words we use;

the psychological level, the 'subtext', is the meaning we give to the words through our tone of voice, body language or the expression on our face.

For example, if someone was to say, 'Nice shoes,' it could mean just that: that they like the shoes you're wearing (social meaning). But if they said it in a sarcastic tone of voice it could mean the exact opposite, even though the words are the same (psychological meaning). It's the psychological level that indicates the speaker's ego state, so in this example they're likely to be in Critical Parent Negative (it's a put-down; or maybe they think they're the wrong colour shoes for this occasion) or Adapted Child Negative (jealous of your cool shoes).

What is the most important indicator of ego state? Think back to Mehrabian and his findings about congruence, and the relative importance of verbal, vocal and visual in how we are perceived. What we say, the words we use, is low down in terms of influence; vocal (how we sound) and visual (how we look) are more reliable indicators of ego state.

The written word can be very dangerous because – unless it's very expertly done – it only tells part of the story. That's why face-to-face presentation is still such a key part of business pitches, and the written supporting document alone isn't enough; and that's why emails can create so much misunderstanding and ill-feeling, and why emoji have become so popular: to try to convey the *feeling* behind the words.

How can I recognise the different ego states?
Different looks and sounds signify different states in different people, although the table a few pages back will give you some idea of what to look out for.

A lot of the time, people are out of control of the way they come over and the impact they make: their look and sound don't match their intention. It's not deliberate. As part of taking more control of your own ego states, it's helpful to remember that people's apparent behaviour towards you, their reactions to you, can be deceptive: they may have nothing to do with you at all. **If they appear to be angry or irritated, it isn't necessarily about you.**

What puts us into a particular ego state?
Ego states are not fixed or plodding; we move round the TA House the whole time, and can switch between rooms at lightning speed

and for no apparent reason. This is because our ego states are determined by a complex combination of influences at varying levels of consciousness, from our early childhood through to something somebody said to us thirty seconds ago.

It's not my place to get into a deep psychological analysis of all of this. I just want to focus on a couple of practical things that will help you 'in the heat of the moment' of a conversation, and give you just enough background understanding of TA theory to support that. If you want to find out more about TA, there are some great books about it. (As a starting point, I strongly recommend *Transactional Analysis in Organisations* by Keri Phillips – it's short and clear, a great introduction to the subject.)

Can we control our ego states at all?
A lot of the time it can feel like other people put us into a particular ego state, or a particular room in the House. The Parent wagging their finger, speaking in a harsh tone of voice, can push us into tearful, resentful or hard-done-by Adapted Child. The more the Child displays this behaviour, the more the Parent wags, and so it goes on. And on... In fact, this sort of parallel transaction (see how this interaction is depicted in the diagram below: the lines run *parallel* to each other) can carry on indefinitely, until something changes to disrupt the pattern. This is a stuck dynamic, a stalemate, and over time it will define the relationship.

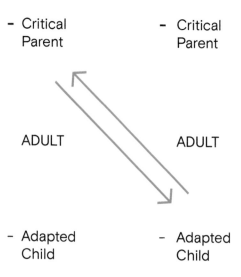

- Critical
  Parent

- Critical
  Parent

ADULT

ADULT

- Adapted
  Child

- Adapted
  Child

When we find ourselves in these situations, it seems as if the way we feel and behave is being provoked by the behaviour of the other person. After all, feeling defensive is a perfectly normal response to a wagging finger, isn't it? In the same way, feeling inadequate and helpless, or maybe frustrated, rebellious and reckless (AC−), is an understandable response to someone who smothers you with help to the extent that you can't do anything for yourself and feel shut down – the negative Nurturing Parent.

But the key thing to remember in all of this is that, despite how it may feel at the time, **you do have a choice**. You can *choose* how you respond to other people. You can cower away from a wagging finger – but you can also (and this is just one of many options) get angry and fight back. You might feel patronised, inadequate and useless when faced with someone who's being overly 'helpful'; alternatively you could choose to go on a reckless spree of glorious irresponsibility.

All these responses are just perpetuating the relationship though: they encourage the other person to stay in the same ego state. They are parallel transactions. But there is a response you can adopt that will break this gridlock: you can move into Adult. This will set up a 'crossed transaction' (see how the lines in the diagram below are no longer parallel but cross each other?) that will break the established pattern of the transaction. Breaking the old pattern and getting into a new one may not happen immediately; the other person may stay stuck in their old negative ego state for some time, even forever. But if you stay in Adult for long enough, chances are they'll eventually come and join you in there, and you can enjoy some real understanding and come to a positive resolution.

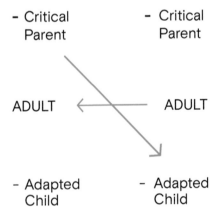

- Critical
Parent

- Critical
Parent

ADULT

ADULT

- Adapted
Child

- Adapted
Child

As an example:

CP–: 'Why do you always waste everyone's time with your incessant questions?'

AC– might respond by falling silent, feeling thoroughly put down and embarrassed (and possibly seething with anger and resentment). Instead, a disarming Adult reply might be: 'I don't mean to waste anyone's time and I'm sorry if I haven't made my intention clear. I'm just trying to get some clarity that I think is important and would be useful to us all.'

Another essential starting point for staying in positive ego states or in Adult is the notion of **unconditional positive regard** (UPR). This is a term credited to humanistic psychologist Carl Rogers. Practising UPR means accepting and respecting others as they are without judgement or evaluation, and this is a prerequisite of getting into the Adult space. Reflect for a moment on the times when your behaviour and response to someone have been driven by some preconceived perception of them, or a memory of them from a previous encounter, or some subconscious association that they trigger in you but which really has nothing to do with them (you may wish to refer back to any notes you made from the exercise you did on this subject back in Chapter 2). If you're anything like me, this can happen a lot; and I always find that my interactions are much more positive and productive if I stay in the moment and take people 'as I find them'.

UPR applies to you too: to get the best from an interaction, you need to enter it with positive esteem for yourself – self-esteem – as well as positive esteem for the other person. Before you go in, think yourself into a mindset of 'I'm OK; you're OK' or I+U+. This is an easy thing to say, but a tough thing to do! It means you have to free yourself from the distorting influences and unconscious bias of negative Parent injunctions and Child emotions, and these can take a lot of working out. But it's well worth making a habit of. Being rooted in Adult is a strong place to be.

Imposter syndrome

I've found that You brand and an understanding of TA can be very helpful in breaking down imposter syndrome: the usually baseless feeling of being unworthy, out of place, a fake, shouldn't really be there … It's very widespread, even at senior levels.

Here are two short client case studies …

'I never realised why I had imposter syndrome or where it came from, but after spending time with Julia and her team I worked out that it came from my careers teacher at school telling me I'd never amount to anything because I talked too much, and later a boss telling me I was presenting 'wrong' in front of my client, which made me fearful of ever presenting again. I present and speak for a living, so those two incidents have haunted me for years. The realisation came during a session with Julia. It was like an epiphany, like "OMG! *That's* why I'm always looking over my shoulder, waiting for someone to tell me I'm no good or I've done it wrong", like a lightbulb switch. It was when I was preparing my piece to camera for the end of the day – a true lightbulb moment. Imposter syndrome still comes to say hello sometimes, but now I never let it stay. I look at it and close the door on it!'
Victoria O'Farrell, MD, Motivational Voice Ltd.,
BAWE Board Member

And here's something written by Mark, a director in a communication consultancy firm, that gives some interesting insights:

'For much of my life I've had a fear of being found out. Not for anything specific or something I've done particularly, but because of feeling generally and vaguely unable to live up to expectations (whether mine or other people's I've never been sure). Some of this was probably a psychological accident of birth; but it was probably topped up, I think, by feeling only average in institutions that the rest of the world regard as exceptional (Cambridge University, MBA school).

I've done some research into this feeling, and found that 'imposter syndrome' is well documented. And it's widespread, even (perhaps particularly) at senior levels in the business, professional and political worlds. At its heart lies a fear of exposure. This shows up in all sorts of different ways and provokes a wide range of responses. Some people become over-achievers, never satisfied with who they are or what they've done, driving themselves on relentlessly to 'the next thing'. Personally I opted for avoidance and self-effacement, hiding my nagging feeling of inadequacy behind false modesty, cynicism and a deflecting humour. If that sounds like a carefully worked out plan, believe me, it wasn't. But it had a significant impact on the way I communicated and engaged with people:

I deliberately avoided situations where there was a chance of being asked to 'say a few words'; I'd go red (or felt I did) if I was asked a question or in any way singled out in front of people ... even one to one, I became apprehensive that uncontrolled self-consciousness could ambush me at any time.

Now please don't think I presented myself the whole time as a gibbering wreck. Far from it. I became practised at the art of deception. I relied a lot on intellectual processes and the written word ('incisive analysis, great report'). If I had to make a high visibility presentation I'd memorise and rehearse until I was word perfect, and would usually get well reviewed (which if anything just made the whole imposter syndrome and self-esteem thing worse because it reinforced the falsehood).

So I got by. But my day to day performance was pulled down. My contribution to meetings and conversations generally was sometimes unconfident, fragile and shot through with qualification and academic hesitation. And the higher profile set-piece events were always just one more layer of stuff to worry about and plan for, either working out excuses for avoiding them altogether or else putting in a load of prep, always with the background worry that it could all go disastrously wrong. More generally, all of this contributed to a general feeling that I wasn't getting the best out of my career, my life, myself, and that I was missing opportunities because of an amorphous, low level fear that I felt I could do nothing about and just had to accept and 'get on with it'.

It sounds corny to say that the You brand programme changed my life – but it did. It's removed the fear, and that has been
truly amazing. 'Public speaking' has become something that I positively enjoy, and I don't waste a lot of time preparing for it in the way I did. I have a much better understanding of how interactions work, in business meetings and conversations generally, and I'm far more aware now of how I respond and what works and what doesn't. And I like to think I'm more tolerant and accepting of others, because I know how easily people can come across in ways they don't intend; and that if they upset me it's more likely my 'stuff' than theirs anyway.

I'm sure the coaching works in different ways for different people, but for me there were a couple of blinding flashes fairly early on that made a huge shift in my mind set. The first was that, at a certain level, being 'good' at communication is a lot to do with technique, rather than about your intrinsic worth as a person; so it's something you can change significantly without overhauling anything too fundamental in your being. And the second – which seems so obvious now in hindsight – is that not only does the way you feel shape the way you speak, but also the way you speak changes how you feel about yourself. In a sense, as Julia would say, 'you define yourself through expressing yourself.' So You brand coaching has changed my attitudes, approach and responses to things in ways I couldn't have imagined. It's allowed me to seek out opportunities and take on new challenges that a few years ago I would have run a mile from – and which I now positively enjoy.

As for imposter syndrome … I still get flashes of it occasionally, but I have a much higher level of background confidence now that keeps it in check. You might say I'm a bit of an imposter as an imposter these days. It may be partly an age thing, but I'm sure You brand has had a lot to do with it.'

How do I get into Adult?

Basically, with a lot of self-awareness, positive self-criticism, patience and practice. Use unconditional positive regard (I+U+) to put you into an open, receptive frame of mind. Use performance energy and the performance toolkit to help lift you out of the negative ego states into the positive ones; from here it's a relatively short step into Adult. Here are some practical things you can do – in the heat of the moment when you feel your chain is being 'yanked' – to get into Adult. I want you to keep them to the forefront of your mind and actively try them out next time things get sticky…

- Breathe and take a pause: this will help take the heat out of the situation and stop you from knee-jerking into a parallel transaction. You may find it helpful simply to change your position in your chair, or to get up and move about – this will help move you into a different psychological space.
- Remember unconditional positive regard: the other person's behaviour may be a distortion of what they really feel or mean; don't judge them by it. It probably has nothing to do with you in any case.

- Practise ways of crossing a transaction: rehearse saying things like 'I'm interested to hear you say that. I'd like to know more about your thinking here; please will you expand on that a bit?' But avoid doing this in a way that looks or sounds patronising, judgemental or cross. (We'll be looking at some very useful active listening techniques that will help with this.)
- Remember: you have total choice over how you respond to what someone says or their behaviour. They cannot make you feel anything. Your feelings are your own; you control them. In the same way, other people's feelings are their own; you are not responsible for them. In any interaction, you're only responsible for 50%.

'No one can make you feel inferior without your consent.'
Eleanor Roosevelt

- Respond, don't react. When you find what someone is saying challenging or difficult to deal with, connect to your Adult by taking a breath or a pause. Acknowledge what they've said ('Hmmm, that's an interesting point, I'll need some time to think about that'), but don't rise to the bait or in the heat of the moment you may say something you'll later regret. Remember that 50% of it is their stuff.
- Remember that being in Adult doesn't guarantee you'll get what you want. At least not superficially. You'll always be faced with Yes, No or a compromise. All the other ego states, certainly when they're negative, are essentially manipulative, used to get 'what you want'. By contrast, being truly in Adult carries with it a preparedness to let go and to accept the outcome. Even though this may mean foregoing a short-term gain, the likelihood is that it will safeguard and strengthen your relationship with that person into the future – which is a real 'win–win'.

Is Adult always best?
In much of the literature about TA, pure Adult is often held up as *the* thing to shoot for, the only good place to be. However, pure Adult on its own is clinical and unfeeling. If we spent all our time in it we would probably be pretty dull. Don't be afraid of using the other ego states, in their positive aspect, in your interactions with people; just see the Adult state as a way of framing and anchoring them so they are positive and constructive. You can be Free Child *in Adult*, or Nurturing Parent *in Adult*, for example. These can be strong places, and can be used strategically to help shift the person you're talking to, and yourself, into a more positive place.

Your feelings are your own; you control them. Other people's feelings are their own. In any interaction, you're only responsible for 50%.

Maintaining an Adult 'filter' will keep your other ego states positive, and keep you in charge and able to use them at their best, rather than them controlling you.

The idea of being Positive Parent or Child 'in Adult' is central to what are known as **bull's-eye transactions**, which are the most solid underpinning to the Adult state. In order to fully engage someone, it's important that you appeal to them on a variety of different levels: to their Values (Parent), Sense (Adult) and Feelings (Child). If any of these is missed, you will only get partial engagement: people may agree to an idea because it excites them (Child) only to change their minds later because it doesn't accord with their values (Parent). 'Let's make loads of money (Yes! Excited Child) selling arms (No! Shocked Parent).' Failure to engage people on multiple levels is the reason why so many of the decisions apparently agreed in meetings subsequently come unstuck.

Bull's-eye transactions happen when there is a free flow of energy between all the ego states, so that you access the values, sense and excitement in someone and get their full 'whole person' engagement – so that people don't sit there nodding 'Yes' with their head when their heart is shouting 'No!', or the other way round. Bull's-eye transactions help people move into the safe Adult space of negotiation and resolution. Harnessing the positive aspect of all the ego states in ourselves is the key to harnessing them in others – this is the touchstone of really great communication.
And the springboard for doing this is? You've guessed it – performing yourself!

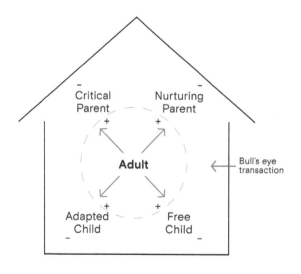

Do I have to remember and know how to 'do' all the words?
That is, the words in the table a few pages back. And the answer is no, certainly not. Trying to get into each of the different states in this way would definitely be cart before horse. The key to performing and projecting each of the states is to be emotionally connected to it; then the authenticity of you and what you are saying will come through. This happens through and because of performance energy. So get connected, turn on the energy, and facial expression, body language and vocal tonality and variety will take care of themselves.

Labelling
As I became more familiar with TA, I realised the extent to which 'labelling' was used to put people into negative ego states.

Early in the 2000s I designed and ran a successful 'Women in Business' programme, which subsequently became part of Theresa May's 'Women to Win' initiative aimed at getting more women elected as MPs. At the time I had recently started to research and use TA as part of the **You brand** methodology, as it seemed to be a perfect fit as a guide to understanding the connection between our physical, vocal and emotional impact: how we look and sound and how people feel about us.

Back then (as now) there was a lot of discussion about how few women sat on company boards. I remember listening to the famous remark Harriet Harman made at a conference: that it is impossible to have joined-up understanding and proper governance when we don't include 50% of the population in the process.

I'd observed in the corporate world how women in senior and middle management often adopt coping strategies in response to what they see – either consciously or subconsciously – as a threatening environment. The threat may come from an ingrained conditioning that defers, probably unconsciously and inexplicitly, to an idea that men have natural authority, certainly in the workplace. Or else it may come from the fact that at this level on the corporate ladder women become a minority (as evidenced, even now in 2020, by the small number of women clients I see).

Any group of people, when they find themselves in a minority, feel threatened and adopt coping strategies to deal with the threat or simply to survive (I've since found there's a lot of research to substantiate this, e.g. Henri Tajfel's Social Identity Theory). These coping strategies will be based on how we are feeling; we use them to help us either to fit in, or deliberately not to fit in, depending on our natural response to threat and whatever we find 'works'.

Whatever our response though, the fact is that these strategies usually prevent us from being who we truly are. And if we as women find ourselves in a predominantly male environment, the strategies (and the behaviour that goes with them) attract and are reinforced by labels – labels that can stereotype and belittle the woman they are attached to. (Men too adopt coping strategies, but on the whole their behaviour is considered the norm, the benchmark, and is immune to labelling).

How are people labelled?
So some women may be 'flirtatious' or 'girly', while others are 'aggressive' (if we dare to stand up to a man who is claiming our idea as his own in a meeting, for example), 'bossy', 'ballbreaker' or 'man in a skirt' (if we show strong leadership), or 'ice maiden' (if we retain our composure and don't join in with an offensive joke). Labelling like this is pernicious, often deliberately hurtful, belittling and bullying, and is used to keep people 'in their place'.

Labelling is almost invariably destructive. Moving beyond my own feelings on the subject (which you can probably tell are strong) and the individual psychological harm it does, labelling – and the scarcity of women at senior levels in corporate and public life that it helps perpetuate – has a massive negative impact on our economy, our politics and our social and psychological welfare generally. There is a huge amount of evidence for this – just Google 'business case for diversity' for some examples.

Labelling is part of an environment and culture that prevent women from being and expressing who they truly are, and that exclude their perspectives, logic, feelings and intuition from shaping the world. It has made many women frightened of their own power, and insecure about expressing it in a natural and authentic way – an insecurity that is perpetuated partly because of a lack of senior women role models. If we're not reflected in an organisation we feel excluded from it. It's one thing for companies and organisations to claim they have a diverse workforce (in terms of gender, age, ethnicity, religion and so on) but unless people feel *genuinely* included in the culture then nothing changes and the bottom line of the business or the effectiveness of the organisation are adversely affected. Having more women in senior roles will allow people – men and women alike – to be more *themselves*, and help create a more authentic culture where people will want to stay.

Although society still operates through a predominantly male lens, I am optimistic that this situation can and will change (for example, the current #MeToo and #TimesUp campaigns are moving things in a positive direction). All women, individually, have the ability to overcome labels and bring their true selves to work. Think about the TA House. All the labels – and the behaviour they describe – map directly onto negative ego states, either Parent or Child. Ballbreaker, Man in Skirt or Ice Maiden are negative Critical Parent; Girly or Flirty are negative Adapted Child; Mummy or Nanny are negative Nurturing Parent; and so on. To break out of these states, and to destroy the labels, all you need do is breathe, shake the mindset, turn on the performance energy and get into Adult. It's simple – when you know how…

 One of my star women in the first Women in Business pilot groups was a 'top cop' from the Met who I'd met at an event for senior policewomen at Scotland Yard. A colleague and I delivered a challenging presentation around the TA model and the basic premise of our work – how people's perception of you is influenced by how you look and sound. The audience was made up of some very intimidating-looking women who I felt were sitting there thinking, 'What the hell is all this fluffy stuff?' It was one of the most daunting sessions I've ever done.

Towards the end Lynda La Plante, an old friend (we had worked as actors together), joined the group, and with great surprise asked me, 'What are you doing here?' She was at that time researching her TV series *Prime Suspect*, and at drinks afterwards she introduced me to the senior police officer who was liaising with her on the show. The woman in question had reached a point in her life when she was a bit cynical and feeling that it was time to retire. Her commander took me aside and said, 'We really don't want her to go, is there anything you can do?' We ended up talking and I eventually threw down the gauntlet and challenged her to come on this new course to help pioneer it.

She accepted. Her brilliance and her ability were not in question, but her confidence and authenticity as a senior policewoman were being challenged by how she felt about herself, and this translated into how she looked and sounded. She felt she couldn't go any further up the ladder, so was retreating. Her demeanour was hunched and introverted and quite scary. Her body language and the tonal quality of her voice (all on one note) didn't demonstrate authority or real leadership. She needed to grow into the very senior leadership role she wanted but wasn't sure she could go for. She came to me for a number of sessions where we worked on her physical presence, her centred Adult connection and showing the strong woman that she was. She went on to become Deputy Assistant Commissioner. I felt very proud.

Once you've got a real sense of how to use TA in the moment with no blood on the carpet, no misunderstanding, resentment or damaged feelings, you will be well on the way to your **You brand.** Using TA and performing yourself through it takes consistent effort and practice (at least that's been my experience) – but boy, is it worth it! In challenging situations it can be a real lifesaver.

Learning about how we work and how we impact on the world is one of the greatest gifts we can give ourselves. Self-awareness is the key to a happy and fulfilled life. It's a source of lasting success, even when you may be feeling less than successful in other more superficial ways.

SUMMARY CHAPTER 12

• It's not just about presentations and set-piece events; how we come across in conversations and meetings also has a big influence on how we are perceived by people. To have a **You brand** we need to perform authentically and consistently (well!) across all these situations.

• Transactional Analysis is a framework for understanding the psychological drivers of interactions between people and our internal interactions with ourselves.

• The TA House is a helpful way of visualising the interplay between the ego states of Parent, Adult and Child.

• Whichever ego state we are in will influence how we look and sound, and thus how people transact with us. The ego state you are in is not dictated by other people – it's *your* choice.

• You are not responsible for other people's feelings – they are their own.

• You are responsible for only 50% of the outcome of an interaction, so be prepared to walk away whatever the outcome with no ill-feeling or blood on the carpet.

• Parallel transactions keep us in a rut; we can break out of them using a crossed transaction. This will almost certainly require a change in our tone of voice, facial expression and body language, as well as (probably) in the words we use.

• The Adult state is the place for real negotiation and resolution. 'Bull's-eye' transactions are the most powerful: where we engage the positive Parent and Child from within the Adult ego state, and accept Yes, No or a compromise as the possible outcomes.

• Being in Adult requires us to have unconditional positive regard for others and ourselves – negative preconceptions about people get in the way.

• Respond, don't react.

• Performance energy and using the Variety Pack will help you break out of negative ego states and get into a rounded Adult place.

Things to work on
For the next week at least, stay with this learning: live with it, try it out and get as comfortable as you can with using it in all your interactions – starting with yourself, of course! Practise in front of the mirror or your camera: see what ego state people would infer from how you look and sound, and see if this aligns with how you're feeling and what you actually intend – and make any necessary adjustments, working these into your muscle memory.

Observe people. Have fun working out where they are in the House. Observe yourself. Monitor what happens to you in different situations and where in the House you go – and try to work out why. What is it that is really driving your response? Is it the reality of the situation, or something that's been programmed into you by years of habit? Whenever you feel you're in a negative place or moving towards one, remember that you have a choice. Breathe, turn on your performance energy and move into a different gear – and observe and feel how this changes things.

A few practical tips to keep front of mind for meetings, and to help you get yourself and others into positive states... Introverts: remember that if you haven't spoken in the first five minutes of a meeting you are not present – and the longer you leave it the harder it is to get back in; and extraverts: make a point of listening, reflecting and thinking more before you speak. If you're chairing a meeting, don't start on 'the business' until everyone has spoken and been acknowledged. In all our company meetings we start with 'Morning News': everyone takes turns in standing and speaking for a minute or two about how they're feeling, what's on their mind, and possibly (but not necessarily) what they want to achieve in the meeting, any concerns they have etc.

Make notes in your **You brand** diary.

CHAPTER 13

You With the 'What': Strategising Your Content

*'If you wish to persuade me, you must think my thoughts,
feel my feelings, and speak my words.'*
Cicero

There are two more pieces of the jigsaw to put in place (remember
the Journey Map in the Introduction?). The first of these is the
'What' – the 7% in the Communication Wheel, the golden bullet.
This is the 'content'. Don't be misled by the 7% figure – to be
golden, your content has to be 100%. Establishing what your
content is is one thing; but *how* you deliver it and strategise the
meaning will determine how it lands and how we feel about it.

Let me introduce you to Aimapping.

Aimapping: Audience and Arena Impact Mapping

This is a strategic planning tool for shaping and focusing you and
your content to target a specific audience and arena. It acts as
a repository and filter through which to run all the factual, linear,
emotional, lateral and physical information about an arena, situation
or audience, and helps you to develop real engagement in yourself
about your subject and to make informed choices about your
audience and your approach.

Imagine your own personal computer into which you can feed all
your chaotic thoughts, concerns, worries, ideas and aspirations
about a forthcoming presentation, event or meeting. You press a
button or two, and out come the answers, the format and the clarity
that will enable you to talk fluently with real purpose and interaction,
with you firmly present and in control. Does that sound like a dream,
too good to be true? Well, with Aimapping, it can be a consistent
reality that can transform your communicating career.

So here it is, in stages – with diagrams!

First we need to establish the 'coat hanger', from which all ideas, questions and challenges will hang. This will determine how our narrative will flow and how it will land.

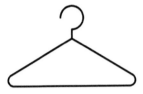

This then is the blank 'storyboard' that we'll fill in as we go. The content of the storyboard comes from working through the Storywheel (look back at Chapter 6 to remind yourself if you need to). But until we hang it from the coat hanger (and feed in the other elements of the Aimap), the storyboard – the output from the Storywheel – is flapping in the breeze; it has no real purpose or direction. The purpose of the Aimap is to fine-tune it and make it acutely relevant to a specific audience and situation.

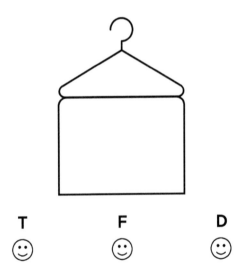

The diagram also shows the people who the story has to connect with and influence: the audience. In strategising your story you need to consider TFD: what you want them to Think, Feel and Do. And you need to do this at every stage of the Aimapping process. An acute awareness of the needs of your audience – or at least your assessment based on the best intelligence you have – and what you're trying to achieve with them are what drive it.

Let's look at the coat hanger in more detail. It starts with 'Theme' and 'Thrust':

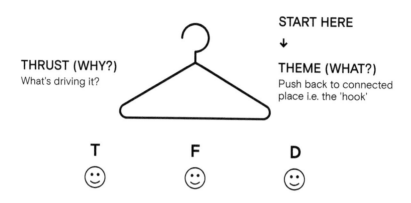

START HERE
↓

THRUST (WHY?)
What's driving it?

THEME (WHAT?)
Push back to connected place i.e. the 'hook'

T   F   D

Theme or Title (What?)

If you've started your Storywheel with a piece of personal disclosure wrapped in an 'I' statement, then you'll be in a good place to pin down your theme or title. If not, you're probably looking at something that's pretty dry and impersonal, something that you don't feel very connected to yourself – let alone your audience.

To work out your title, start with the generic explanatory purpose of the narrative, e.g. 'Health and Safety in the Workplace' or 'The Three-Year Corporate HR Strategy', or some such. Then you need to ask yourself: 'What does this mean to me?' How do you move into engagement and real personal connection with the audience? How do you grab their interest and move them into your world? The first thing is to push back on the generic title and come up with a more personal, more human interpretation of it, a kind of tabloid newspaper headline that gets you onto the path where you can really own it. Pushing back on the HR Strategy title could yield something like 'We need to leverage our talent' – hmmm, a bit better, but it's still not very engaging, is it? Pushing back further: 'Bringing out the best in our people'; and further still: 'We all need to behave differently to bring out the best in ourselves and each other.'

Or another example: if you're talking about 'The Plant's New Health and Safety Initiative', try framing it in a more emotionally connected (and connecting) way: 'This is about saving lives' or just 'Let's keep ourselves safe.'

Push back on yourself until you find the nub of what you want to talk about. Don't worry if what you come up with sounds extreme, so long as it's genuine. When it comes to it, you don't have to actually use these words, but going through the pushback process to clarify and define your real feelings will give focus to how you talk about the subject, and will release the emotional energy you need to speak with real feeling and engage and move people – and persuade them of your argument. It's a way for you to start to find something that really does say what you mean so you can mean what you say. In my experience, the fact that people don't go through this process is why there is so much woolly, bland, unengaging and ineffective communication in the corporate and professional world (and beyond).

Thrust (why?)

Here we start to build our argument and our narrative purpose, filling out the 'because': the reason *why* we have to do whatever we said in the title.

Why is 'The Plant's New Health and Safety Initiative' important? Probably, at one level, because new targets have been handed down from Head Office, and if they're not met the plant will be penalised. While this may be valid as a reason on an intellectual level, it's pretty uninspiring on a personal level: unlikely in itself to change people's behaviour on the shop floor. But if the subtext is 'Look after each other or risk facing a lifetime of loss and regret' the message will be felt much more powerfully.

Spins (how?)

No one likes to feel directly implicated or have the finger pointed at them. Use spins – stories, anecdotes, examples, personal disclosure – to land messages powerfully, but in a non-accusatory way; for example, to illustrate the consequences, positive and negative, of action (or inaction) by reference to other people or situations, and allow people to infer parallels with themselves. Let their imagination do the rest.

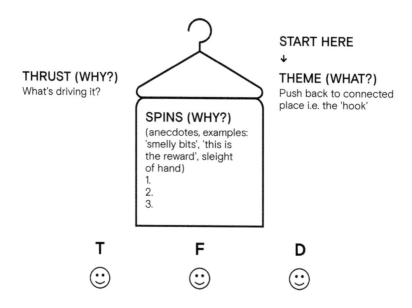

THRUST (WHY?)
What's driving it?

START HERE
↓
THEME (WHAT?)
Push back to connected place i.e. the 'hook'

SPINS (WHY?)
(anecdotes, examples: 'smelly bits', 'this is the reward', sleight of hand)
1.
2.
3.

T   F   D

Spins are a great way of dealing with 'skeletons in the closet' or 'smelly' bits, of softly acknowledging how you've learned from past mistakes, or how brilliantly something you're proposing worked in another situation.

Archetypes or roles
We all have several archetypes, or roles, in our make-up that resonate within us and strongly influence our behaviour and motivations, and the personae we tend to adopt. Here are the ones I find most relevant when I'm coaching:

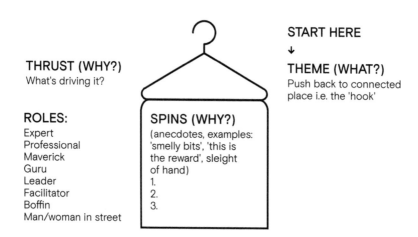

THRUST (WHY?)
What's driving it?

START HERE
↓
THEME (WHAT?)
Push back to connected place i.e. the 'hook'

ROLES:
Expert
Professional
Maverick
Guru
Leader
Facilitator
Boffin
Man/woman in street

SPINS (WHY?)
(anecdotes, examples: 'smelly bits', 'this is the reward', sleight of hand)
1.
2.
3.

Before you go into a meeting, presentation or other interaction, think about which archetype/role to draw on to best suit your purpose with that audience in that situation. This can determine not just behaviour, but also other aspects of how you present yourself, such as what you wear. Do you need/want to be part of the group or outside of it – an observer, or a dominant player? Think about which archetype will get the best result.

As an aside, of all of them, 'man/woman in the street' is one of the most powerful: it gives you easy access in all sorts of different situations; people will often disclose more readily because they don't feel threatened by you and they'll tend to listen to you more because you somehow represent the impartial voice of reason and common sense.

Tactics

Think about where you stand vis-à-vis your audience in terms of age and experience (not hierarchical seniority) and adjust how you approach them accordingly.

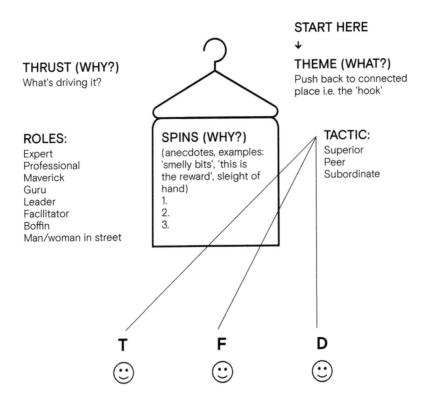

START HERE
↓

THRUST (WHY?)
What's driving it?

THEME (WHAT?)
Push back to connected place i.e. the 'hook'

ROLES:
Expert
Professional
Maverick
Guru
Leader
Facilitator
Boffin
Man/woman in street

SPINS (WHY?)
(anecdotes, examples: 'smelly bits', 'this is the reward', sleight of hand)
1.
2.
3.

TACTIC:
Superior
Peer
Subordinate

T   F   D

The following tactics are useful:

Peers: talk about 'we' and 'us'. NB this isn't the 'royal We'. It's about shared human experience: 'We all know how it feels to...', e.g. have had a sleepless night because of a crying baby, feel elated by a piece of good news.

Superiors: 'stroke' them; acknowledge their greater experience: 'I know you have huge experience in this, but...' – this will make them more receptive to your point of view.

Subordinates: don't patronise. Avoid things like 'I remember when I was your age' or 'I know what it feels like...' – these are an instant turn-off! Instead, give them a story from your own experience at their age, and let them draw their own parallels. Use confident, humorous but powerful personal disclosure (look back to Chapter 6 if you need a reminder).

The tactic you adopt will have a direct impact on your audience's TFD.

Think, Feel and Do: TFD
Everything about what you say, how you say it and the way you come over needs to be geared to the outcome you want: what do you want your audience to Think based on how they Feel and consequently what will they go away and Do as a result of their interaction with you? Remember that how influential you are depends on how people feel about themselves when they're with you.

Think
What's the first thing you want people to say to each other or themselves as they leave the meeting, presentation or conversation?

Our feelings are much stronger determinants of our response than our conscious thoughts, and largely determine what and how we remember. What your audience thinks about you will be driven largely by how they feel about you...

Feel
Remember: in You brand, you are the message. In order to excite people, don't try to be exciting – be excited. The most effective way of frightening someone is not by being frightening, but by being frightened yourself. It's a far stronger way of communicating

You are the message. In order to excite people, don't try to be exciting – be excited. You have to inhabit the emotion.

emotion; but it means, of course, that you have to be totally – and visibly – immersed in the feeling yourself. You have to inhabit the emotion.

Do

There are broadly four types of response you can get from an audience in terms of what they go away and do as a result of listening to you: 'Yes'; 'No'; 'I'll think about it'; 'I'd like to know more about it.' Be realistic about what you can achieve. If you shoot for a 'Yes' too early you risk blowing everything. Just getting people going away *thinking* takes a lot of doing. This must be a driver right through the Aimapping process. It makes you push back on your thinking to take into account the actual reality of the audience, and it forces you to find out and work out more about them.

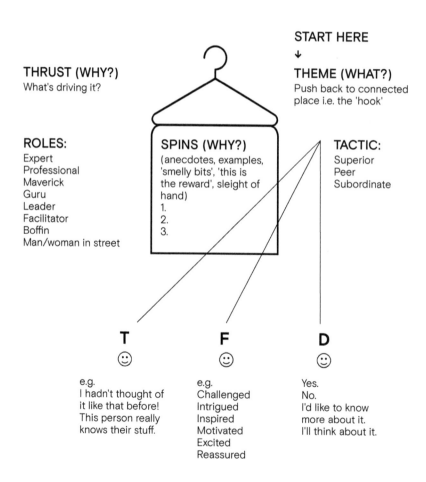

START HERE
↓

THRUST (WHY?)
What's driving it?

THEME (WHAT?)
Push back to connected place i.e. the 'hook'

ROLES:
Expert
Professional
Maverick
Guru
Leader
Facilitator
Boffin
Man/woman in street

SPINS (WHY?)
(anecdotes, examples, 'smelly bits', 'this is the reward', sleight of hand)
1.
2.
3.

TACTIC:
Superior
Peer
Subordinate

T
☺
e.g.
I hadn't thought of it like that before! This person really knows their stuff.

F
☺
e.g.
Challenged
Intrigued
Inspired
Motivated
Excited
Reassured

D
☺
Yes.
No.
I'd like to know more about it.
I'll think about it.

Assess where the audience is in their process of persuasion to you and your argument. You are building the argument through 'What' and 'Why'; and you are *always* putting forward an argument, which is shaped by your decisions and strategy about how you approach the audience and how this interacts with their beliefs and response. All of this needs to be brought together and decided upon, and this will determine which 'Do' to shoot for. The normal tendency is to throw everything at the wall and hope that some of it sticks – but you can be much smarter.

By the time you've finished, the Aimap should look something like the one above (but with choices made and everything filled in, of course). Actually mine nearly always look a complete mess, full of squiggles, crossings-out and adjustments – but all of these are a necessary part of the creative process, of defining and deciding on all the aspects of your message.

Working through and completing your Aimap will give you a much clearer idea of what you want to say, how you should say it and what reaction and response you can hope to get. And you'll probably find that your perspective and approach shift as different parts of the Aimap interact with each other, opening up new considerations and possibilities that will refine your understanding and your approach to the situation. You may well find for example, as you work through it, that what you put down as a 'Spin' is in fact more powerful as the 'Thrust' (plot); so don't be afraid to adjust and move things around. If you're working in a team, the Aimap is a great way of opening up valuable discussion and exchange of ideas and information, some of which probably wouldn't come to light without going through this process.

 Trying Out Your Aimap
Once you've worked through your Aimap, take a short break. Then go back over it and put down the key pontoons that have emerged from the process – you'll probably find that some surprising things have revealed themselves and have become vital triggers for your narrative. Limit yourself to about six pontoons and remember to use short, simple, descriptive colloquial words. Look back at Chapter 7 for a reminder of how to record your pontoons.

Now set up your camera and up you get! Making full use of the Variety Pack (louder/softer, faster/slower; giving the key words emphasis and using pause to build clarity and purpose), step into the performance zone: twice the energy you feel comfortable with from the start (it will always feel a bit weird, but now you know it works). Get on that mini-trampoline in your imagination and go! Do two to three minutes, no more. Keep the pace slow and considered, with plenty of energy. Give yourself time to think and decide how you want a word or phrase to land. The process of assimilation from your Aimap will start to emerge and power your argument and your energy and purpose in delivering it.

Now play it back. Take notes. Are you convinced? Are you interested? Are you impressed by your performance? Do you believe in you? If you can tick all these boxes, then well done. If not, go back and do it again, making whatever adjustments you think necessary. Use different words, bring in more examples, anecdotes and analogies – anything that helps the emotional and visual understanding and clarity: we need to see it in our mind's eye. This will then bring real sense to your narrative and underline your argument and its authenticity.

Ideally, perform it to a friend. At the end, ask them what they think, feel and would be likely to do (TFD), and check this against what you intended in your Aimap. If there's any disparity, work out where this stems from and make whatever adjustments are needed.

Do it again, this time simplifying it. Keep at it until the pathway of your argument and narrative is crystal clear and you feel truly involved, included, and yes, maybe even inspired. The more you give it the better it will be – provided your freedom is contained and supported within a clear structure. 'Freedom within a Framework' at all times!

So far all of this has been theoretical, but in order for Aimapping to work it must have real purpose and relevance to something that is important to you. So take some time to think about an event, a dialogue, a meeting or conversation that you need to have – especially if there's one you've been putting off. This could be a personal matter or a business imperative such as a pitch, presentation or webinar. Here are just some of the areas where Aimapping can give you very practical support:

• Making a presentation
• Putting together a winning pitch
• Preparing for a negotiation, or a difficult or challenging conversation

- Focusing and unblocking the energy within your team
- Selling an idea to a senior person
- Positioning yourself as a leader
- Preparing for an interview or media appearance
- Conducting a performance review that's constructive without pulling punches

Now do a simple Storywheel to start the process of ownership and structuring a pathway, using as your start point an 'I' statement with personal disclosure (of course). Then put that through the Aimapping 'computer', feeding in all the additional contextual information that the process requires about the arena, the audience and your relationship to it. Out will come something that will land and resonate, and provide you with a framework and a narrative pathway that is always flexible and can be fine-tuned to suit a variety of different audiences depending on your analysis of TFD. With practice, you'll find it a simple but very effective tool.

The most important part of this is to 'get it out of your mouth': hear it, see it (if possible) and practise. If it simply stays in your head, even as a beautifully thought-out and intellectually credible monologue, it will never come alive and will reach no one, at any level.

Checking the emotional negotiation: Aimapping and the TA House

You can deepen your work with Aimapping by bringing in considerations you've learned from the Transactional Analysis section in the previous chapter.

In your You brand diary, draw up your TA House and look at any cross-transactions that you can anticipate. Remember, these are the transactions where we break an established pattern and respond from an Adult place, jolting the other person out of any negative ego state they may be in. How does your 'script' accommodate any of the possible negative ego state traps that you can fall into and that will stop you from getting to an agreeable 'Yes'/'No'/compromise in Adult? This will play into and influence how people receive your message. Negativity in your tone of voice, any visual tells, a lack of congruence between how you feel and what you are saying, the actual words you use – all of these can have a major and damaging impact on the way your message comes across. Look back at the matrix of facial, physical and tonal expressions in the chapter on TA and push back on where any energy block is coming from in your House.

This process can be done the other way round too. Examine your TA relationship with your audience first, then do Aimapping; this will establish an authentic and congruent strategy. If there is any block, this process will reveal it and flush it out, which should persuade you to look again at what your real impact and purpose are, so that the message is clear and lands according to the audience's needs. It will help you to get it right and truthful and create flow, which is key.

SUMMARY CHAPTER 13

• Aimapping is a strategic planning tool for your content. It helps you capture and process lateral as well as linear information, and gives you an emotional context to accurately target a given audience.

• The Aimap considers Title, Thrust, Spins, Archetypes/Roles and Tactics. It turns a generic story (produced with the Storywheel) into something specifically targeted to a particular audience and situation.

• You need to gear everything you do to what you want your audience to Think, based on how they Feel and consequently what you can reasonably expect them to go away and Do as a result of their interaction with you.

• Transactional Analysis (TA) can be used to deepen your use of Aimapping.

Things to work on
Use Aimapping! Keep using it! The more you use it, the more instinctive the process will become, and the more it will feed your intuition about situations.

CHAPTER 14

Learning to Listen

'If you really listen you will always know what to say.'
Professor Simon Baron-Cohen

Right. We're all prepared, practised and ready to go. But...

What we still need to look at is the silent partner in this methodology: your ears. To communicate really effectively, you need to *listen*. Neuroscience tells us that human beings aren't actually programmed to listen. We're only programmed to 'take turns', to wait for our chance to speak. How many times have you said something you felt to be important and just known that it has landed on deaf ears? It's at best annoying, at worst hurtful and demoralising.

 I'd like you to think about, and write down in your **You brand** diary, when it was you last genuinely felt really listened to. What was the conversation about? How did it feel?

Or do it the other way round: how did it feel the last time you felt you *weren't* listened to?

For many of us the last time we felt listened to might seem like a lifetime ago. But we are all, at times, guilty of not listening properly – even if we think of ourselves as good listeners. It's very easy to use the time when someone else is talking to either go off into our own reveries, segue off onto a tangent prompted by what someone has just said, or just bide our time till we can interrupt and say what *we* want to say. If we don't listen and just talk, we'll only hear stuff we already know; we won't learn anything new. But it's only by listening *actively* that we'll get full value: we won't just gather information, but we'll be able to pick up undercurrents and subtexts that will allow us to turn that information into *intelligence*, which we can then use. For example, a friend might tell us that they're suicidally depressed because they've lost their job and have no money. If we take this at face value we might respond by reassuring them that they're bound to get another job soon, that money isn't everything, or offering to lend them some money to tide them over. If however we used active listening techniques to push back (gently and sensitively of course), they might reveal that the real cause of their depression is a deep concern that they'll lose their status and the respect and love of their family and friends because they have no job. Drilling down to this level of intelligence – rather than simply relying on superficial information – will make our response to the situation radically different.

So how do we train ourselves to listen, given that it doesn't come naturally? And what are the key techniques of active listening? I use a process I call 'learning the ROPES'.

Learning the ROPES
ROPES is an acronym that stands for:

R = Reflect back. Repeat back a key word or phrase that you've just heard from the other person (listen out for which words they emphasise as this is a good indication of what is important to them). Do this in a neutral, non-judgemental tone, with a slight rising inflection (a lift at the end) to indicate you're asking for confirmation or clarity. This technique achieves three things:
• It invites the speaker to give you additional information, to expand on what they've said.
• It demonstrates that you are listening to what they've been saying.
• It gives you time to think before responding.

O = Open questions, not closed ones that invite the answer 'Yes' or 'No'. It can be surprisingly hard to think of open questions in the heat of the moment, so the TED formula is very useful here: 'Tell me…'; 'Explain a bit about…'; or 'Describe to me…' With any of these you will:
• gain further revelation and understanding.
• demonstrate you are interested in the person, and really listening rather than trying to close down what they are saying or pull them into your own agenda.
• keep the dialogue going so you can find out the real problem or critical information that you need, and clues as to how to interpret it.
• help the person open up and articulate what is bothering them or needs clarification.

P = Paraphrasing: summarising what you have just heard in your own words: 'So as I understand it, the situation is that...' From this you will gain clarification of what the person really means, or further factual information: 'No, that's not right, *this* is what I'm saying...' or 'Yes, that's exactly it, and what's more...' Either of these responses will encourage further discussion and revelation, and demonstrate that you are really listening – as indeed you will have to, because in order to paraphrase you have to concentrate. And the other person will almost certainly feel good and that they're making a connection with you, so it's great for building the relationship.

E = Emotional kite-flying: occasionally push back on the speaker to get a clearer sense of the emotion and feeling behind what they're saying. This is essential if you're to get an accurate understanding of what's really going on. Use phrases like: 'I get a sense that...'; 'You seem to be angry/happy/frustrated about this...' This will encourage disclosure and emotional clarity: either 'Yes, that's exactly it,' or if you're wrong, 'No, that isn't how I feel; what I actually feel is...' Either way, you will get more information and insight into what's going on.

And last but by no means least...

S = Silence. Most of us feel compelled to 'fill the pause'. Instead, try staying neutral, quiet and interested, and let the silence hang. It's likely that the other person will speak (and feel listened to as a result), or you will both feel you've reached a reflective, Adult state of having heard each other. Holding the moment can be very powerful: it's the grown-up or the emotional pause. But it mustn't be aggressive – it should simply be a 'being' moment for sharing respect and giving each other value. Silence allows people to find a solution for themselves.

Underlying all of these techniques is one golden mantra for effective listening: park your own agenda and be interested! The true listening process requires us to curb the impulse to solve, oppose, give our point of view or try to steer the other person in the direction we want them to go. We need to suspend judgement and, as far as we can, get inside their thoughts and feelings and see things from their perspective. Only by doing this can we really understand. Interest, genuine interest, is the path to empathy.

These skills can make an enormous difference to the quality of an actual conversation or dialogue; but they can also be used to introduce a conversational style into a situation where the audience doesn't actually reply or respond in direct interaction, such as in a pitch or presentation. Asking the audience an open or rhetorical question – and building in a pause to let it land – can produce an interactive energy that is very vital and inclusive, and demonstrates that you have the confidence and the ability to bring the audience to you. Emotional kite-flying can work in these 'one-way' situations too: 'I get a sense that some of you…' It makes things more personal and intimate, and demonstrates that you have prepared and done your homework on them, as does 'What this means for you in the Operations Team, or for you, Peter, is…'

Rapport-building is another challenge that can make us feel uncomfortable. Most people know it's something they *should* do, but find it hard or don't quite know how. Many business people see rapport-building as a discrete activity, something you allocate the first few moments of a meeting to before moving on to the matter in hand: 'How was your trip here?/Did you have a good holiday?/How's the hotel? Right, now what I wanted to talk about was…' In fact, real rapport-building is something that happens throughout a meeting or conversation, through what we disclose about ourselves and how we listen and interact with the other person even as we're talking 'business'.

I've often watched clever young consultants, possibly because they're over-focused on 'giving value', coming in and being – excuse the imagery – 'sick on the desk'. By which I mean telling the other person everything they want them to know before having even engaged them in any kind of interaction.

Instead of this, use TED (look back to 'Open questions' in 'ROPES' for a reminder) to start the conversation – or Silence, and let them fill the gap, if that seems more appropriate – and then use other elements of ROPES to build relaxation and personal connection and show genuine interest in the other person. If we aren't given the opportunity to show who we are or encouraged to do so, then nothing of value will really be heard or felt. And as we know, with the passing of time we *only* remember how we felt.

 These skills of course need to be practised. If you possibly can, try out using ROPES with anyone willing and supportive. Then teach them the techniques and reverse the exercise. The key is to encourage them to think of something that they would like to get off their chest, or that they feel a bit challenged by. Use TA to establish this if you can – it works well as a trigger. Film the conversation, play it back and notice how using ROPES changes the impact of you as the listener and deepens the dialogue into something much more productive, revealing and fulfilling. You'll find that your personal gravitas rises considerably, and the rapport between the two of you is deepened.

In order to use ROPES you really do have to listen. I think you'll be amazed by what you learn and how it transforms and adds value to all the previous work you've been doing through this book.

SUMMARY CHAPTER 14

• Listening is a challenging but vital part of the communication process. It is a powerful way of building rapport and gaining useful intelligence about a person or situation.

• Use the ROPES acronym to remember the various listening techniques you can use.

• Rapport-building is something that happens *throughout* a meeting or conversation, even as we're talking 'business', not separately.

• The golden rule of listening is to park your own agenda and be interested!

Things to work on
As ever, practise and observe. And record your experiences – what works well and less well – in your You brand diary. Don't feel you have to use all of ROPES all at once; try it out bit by bit. I always find TED very useful in the heat of the moment, and also find that a lot of the other techniques follow on quite naturally from this. You may feel quite exposed using ROPES to start with – this is perfectly normal. Work on it – it's worth it.

CHAPTER 15

You've Arrived! Where Are You Going?

'Far better is it to dare mighty things, to win glorious triumphs, even though checkered by failure … than to rank with those poor spirits who neither enjoy much nor suffer much, because they live in a grey twilight that knows not victory nor defeat.'
Theodore Roosevelt

I'm often asked by people in the corporate world what is the return on investment from You brand coaching. It's very difficult to quantify, but a 2018 study done by Google into the relative importance of 'soft' skills versus STEM (Science, Technology, Engineering, Maths) expertise among its own employees is very revealing: the seven top characteristics of success at Google are all soft skills. STEM comes in dead last. The study concludes: 'We desperately need the expertise of those who are educated to the human, cultural and social as well as the computational.' Emotional intelligence, understanding and acceptance of difference, collaboration, the inclusion of people and thoughts and ideas are essential in creating a good environment. A culture where people wish to not only stay, but also evolve and create, needs these skills, nowadays probably more than ever. In fact, if and when the current forecasts are borne out, 99% of jobs will be taken by Artificial Intelligence and robotics, with the remaining 1% that are immune to automation falling to people who are creative, adaptable, flexible and open to learning. Emotional intelligence, the ability to have complex social interactions, and leadership that collaborates to build and sustain coherent communities will be in high demand. In terms of employability at least, soft skills such as these will increasingly be hard currency.

Young people coming into the corporate world are going to need a very different environment and culture if we want them to stay; if it's not conducive to how they feel best and work best, they will leave. And they will be of limited value if, as they move into senior

Soft
skills will
increasingly
be hard
currency.

positions, they lack the soft skills that the Google study identified as essential to success.

At an individual level, the concept and experience of **You brand** has had different responses and reactions from people around the world, including:

- This has changed my life!
- It's lifted my career to a whole new level.
- It's given me the courage to change course to find greater fulfilment.
- It's saved my marriage.
- I now accept myself warts 'n' all and know it's OK to be me.
- It's given me the courage and confidence to show up, stand up, speak out... and be me.

Alongside some interesting questions and responses, such as:

- Isn't it egotistical?
- I've always been taught that 'There's no "I" in "team".'
- I'm not that important.
- Who's interested in me?

... to which my answer is always this: although I didn't intend it when I first started out, I have found that **You brand** coaching has significant therapeutic power. This is partly down to the cathartic discipline of performance energy; but another part of it comes from the fact that developing your **You brand** is about discovering and coming to terms with yourself.

'To be that self which one truly is, is indeed the opposite of despair.'
Soren Kierkegaard

I said right at the start that this book would take you on a hero's journey. Was it worth it? Are you seeing the world and your place in it through a different lens? Has your exploration made you stronger, braver? If so, this part of your journey is complete, and you are ready to change the world – or at least be a little bolder in your small corner of it.

Even if you don't want to use your **You brand** to achieve a particular ambition or advance a career in business, politics or the arts, I think you'll find that knowing and accepting who you are – and using and communicating that awareness on an everyday basis – will make you a stronger, more effective and confident human being. If we are to become a better 'us' – as a society, a race – then we have a duty to be brave enough to stand and be counted for the best we can be. If the individual 'I' is strong and brave, then so is the collective 'we' (I like to think of this in theatrical terms: as 'strong individuals in a strong ensemble'). To 'show up', to be 'present', and to engage in active collaboration with those around us is how we can change things and resist the negative and the daunting. It's very hard to bully an assertive and confident person, someone who is true to themselves and ready and able to communicate their brand and to help and inspire others to be brave, visible and true to themselves. Be You, the unique human being you were born to be. If you arm yourself with this truth you can overcome any fear and face any demon.

Now you need to go out into the world and live as your new self: confront your denial and seek out those situations that you may have been avoiding or in which you've been unaware or felt ineffective and frustrated. Self-awareness is the driving force: awareness brings choice, and choice – with the ability to exercise it – brings confidence. Apply what you've learned, and you'll start to see the small, practical everyday things differently. Have that challenging conversation, reframe a difficult relationship, speak up at a meeting, put yourself forward for things, take the stand, mentor other people. Listen to others, and say what you know needs to be said, with the skill and ability to do so to best effect. Having a voice that can be heard and listened to is a jewel beyond price; using it is a personal responsibility.

Take baby steps. It may feel risky at first, but as your confidence grows you'll come to realise it is in fact riskless. A riskless risk. You will be safe. Instead of sidestepping challenging situations you will approach them in a new spirit. It's a spirit that nourishes the key human attributes of courage and resilience, adaptability, empathy, optimism and creativity, and grows our insight into ourselves and others. These are invaluable allies in today's world, helping us to accept uncertainty and insecurity as an opportunity to grow in strength and understanding. I cannot better the advice offered by Tennessee Williams:

"Do what you were created to do. You'll know what this is, because it is what you keep creeping up to, peering at, dreaming of. Do it. If you don't, you'll be punching clocks and eating time doing precisely what you shouldn't, and you'll become mean and you'll seek to punish any and all who appear the slightest bit happy, the slightest bit comfortable in their own skin, the slightest bit smart. Cruelty is a drug, as well, and it's all around us. Don't imbibe."

Practise, practise, practise. Keep learning. Use your new awareness and knowledge, grow your experience and accept the opportunities that come your way to try out your new skills; and before you know it, people will start giving you spontaneous feedback – they will remember you, they'll be enriched through meeting you, you will prosper and become happier. I guarantee it. Take the jump and the parachute will open; you'll land safely and you will have the motivation to do more and more as you feel the buzz. You will become more of yourself, with skill, as your **You brand** encircles you – and becomes you.

ACKNOWLEDGEMENTS

There are lots of people I wish to thank.

First, those who have influenced me in my life, and who have thus, unwittingly, contributed to this book. Whether they have been actual mentors, or people who, on reflection, have been powerful role models, they make an interesting list. They are mostly women, and they all have something unusual in common. I want to thank:

My mum, Pearl, for her adventurous spirit, her courage and passion to lead a creative life and her unique talent for bringing people to life through her acute observation and gift of storytelling. At seventeen she went to London, alone and with no agent, determined to be an opera star. She sang four shows a day and lived in a hostel in Greek Street, on her own and being looked after by the local prostitutes. She served in the Land Army in the Second World War, then stepped out of her working-class background in Chichester to join Joan Littlewood as a co-founder of Theatre Workshop. At one time she ran a smallholding in Sussex, bringing up three daughters and hand-milking a herd of forty cows twice a day so we had a roof over our heads while my dad painted. She published her first book of memoirs of her childhood and early life in Chichester at seventy and put on the first exhibition of her painting at ninety-seven. It sold out.

Marion Lombard, the ballet and modern dance teacher in Chichester who excited and terrified us in equal measure.

My Auntie Jill, independent, alone (she lost both her husband and son in the War), reassuring, organising – and my greatest fan. I loved her. At sixty-eight she bought herself a motorbike, and went by bus to pick it up and ride it home – never having been on one before!

Joan Littlewood, who was always part of my life and whose work and maverick philosophy were instrumental in shaping my independent ways of looking at the world of theatre and ensemble playing – on stage and off.

216

Julia Goodman, my great-great-grandmother, who was a prolific and accomplished Victorian portrait painter. She exhibited at the Royal Academy. She had seven children, including Walter, the acclaimed painter, illustrator and author.

Sister Lawrence, my formidable headmistress, who wielded a power that challenged every fibre of my independent nature.

Cis Berry, the most brilliant voice coach of her generation. She would come into class at drama school like a whirlwind of energy, vitality and positivity. She electrified me. Her style helped me become the coach I am today. She was still working at the RSC and the National Theatre at the age of ninety.

And of course **Maggie Thatcher!** Because she was a *woman* who led a country and told me I could start a business and buy my own house (which I did).

And lastly my **dad**, a fine painter, designer and entrepreneur, who always believed in my right to be me and gave me real insight into the creative process and the world of business.

What is it they all have in common? They were all passionate and courageous women pioneers (except my dad!) who had to take on huge responsibility, sometimes just to earn a living, and work very hard to follow their dream – even more so than women today. But they found their passion and drove it through to the end, even if that end was not always a happy one. They gave me something to look up to and aspire to, and they instilled in me the strength to fight for what I believe in and to never give up. I thank them all from the bottom of my heart.

Over the years many other marvellous people have supported and challenged me and given me opportunities and insights that have stoked a real courage to 'put myself out there' and make things happen – without them I might have found myself rather isolated.

My husband **Mark** has been the rock on which I have built my business, and his brilliant analytical skills have been a constant source of support in the writing of this book. He did the line drawings.

To my 'You brand' coaches, Helena, Lara, Cat and Patricia, and everyone in the Personal Presentation team.

Heartfelt thanks to **Helena Michell** for all her skill, insight, patience, calm, tireless industry, enthusiasm and dedication to 'the Work'.

Lara Danobeitia, who has been with me since the early days of the business and has grown into an inspirational coach. She has been a dedicated member of the team throughout the journey and is a huge support to her clients.

Catriona Elliott Winter, who always brings herself to the team and the work, is courageous and is never afraid to challenge – or indeed be challenged!

Patricia Rodriguez, the newest member, for her courage, intelligence and good sense. She promises to be a great asset to the Company.

Richard Bates, Kate Harper, Robert Shaw Cameron, Andrew Macbean, Patrick Poletti, Elizabeth Moynihan: my committed and brilliant role-player/facilitators – always great fun to work with my theatrical troupe.

Hannah Gernon, who has really run the business for the last twenty years, successively as a young woman, married woman, mother of two... and who has never given up on us, even when things were as bad as they could get. She has always been there. Thank you.

My daughter **Olivia** (who maintains she brought *me* up), whose empathic skills are second to none. Olivia continues the family tradition of creative entrepreneurship: she's about to launch a range of botanical oils for beauty, health and wellbeing. @ols_botanical_blends.

My son **David**, who has inherited some of my madness and, with his ability to see and hold the big picture in his head and to drive himself beyond the normal, has supported me in my thinking since he was a small boy. He is now the company's brilliant brand strategist (when he's not working at his own company XYZ EXCHANGE, a sustainable supply chain platform in the fashion industry).

I'm immensely proud of both of them for playing their part in building a happier world.

Thank you **Christian Küsters** for your excellent guidance on the design of this book and its cover, as on our corporate identity and websites over the years.

Barbara Nassisi for the infographics, and for her diligence, patience and good humour.

Eleanor Rockett @eleanorrockett for her digital marketing genius.

And all the team at **Matador** for their expertise, support and advice.

My special thanks go to my writing mentor, **Philippa Pride,** whose writing course in a yurt in Turkey was a major inspiration to embark on this project. Philippa is editor at Hodder & Stoughton exclusively for Stephen King's books, so I feel very privileged to be part of that stable, and to have enjoyed her incisive advice and support throughout this project.

Last but not least, huge thanks to the many courageous and generous **clients** I have worked with over thirty years, who have been a constant source of inspiration and learning. Too many to mention by name – you know who you are.

I hope you've enjoyed this book
and found it useful.

To register your book and enjoy
discounts on other great You brand
products - including the *You brand:
Confident Anywhere* video
masterclass series - please go to
www.youbrand.com/anywhere

For details of our in person and virtual
coaching services please visit
www.youbrand.com

**YOU
BRAND°**

**YOU
BRAND
TEAMS**

**YOU
BRAND
ANYWHERE**